YOU TOO CAN WORK MIRACLES

Dr. Samuel Ekundayo

DEDICATION

This book is dedicated to you dear reader. I pray that you will live to your fullest potential and fulfil God's purpose for your life. Amen!

ACKNOWLEDGEMENTS

Firstly, I thank God for giving me the revelation of His word, as the central tenet of this book has helped me on my journey of purpose fulfilment. To my Dudushewa and Treasure, I thank you for your love, encouragement, and companionship. You are my purpose partner for life. And to my parents (biological and spiritual), mentors and guides God has placed over me, thank you for all you have done and still doing to stir me in the right direction. I will always be grateful.

Special thanks to Pastor Sam Adetiran for helping me edit the book, and my beloved Opeoluwa Adebakin for the scintillating book cover.

TABLE OF CONTENTS

INTRODUCTION

She could barely talk. In fact, because of this disability, it will not be strange to label her deaf and dumb. But the truth is, she is neither. She was just in need of an intervention or help, a miracle of some sort. Her parents had tried everything caring parents would. They took her to native doctors and nothing positive seemed to materialise from their efforts. They almost gave up, until they met my mother.

Jyothi – my mother, a gifted teacher from Dharwas in Himachal Pradesh, a remote town in India – decided to take her in on account of her parents' plea. She was a renowned teacher in Dharwas. Everyone said she was naturally gifted and described her as having 'special powers.' When it comes to imparting knowledge and transforming the lives of her students, my mother was well known. As far as I know, she had no diabolical means of doing her job; however, you could tell she poured her heart and soul into it.

Prior to taking the girl in, we were told that several teachers had given up on her. No one wanted to accept her under their tutelage, not to talk of attempting to teach her. She had been labelled as unteachable, dull, and hopeless, but my mother did not buy all of that. She took her in and within three months, the girl began talking; reading, and chanting poems louder than anyone ever heard her do. All of that was accomplished by her sheer enthusiasm to learn and do all she was being told to do.

Nobody believed it. Many people visited the school to see the girl. The teachers who had tried with no success, and the native doctors who had failed on her case could not wait to see for themselves. You guessed it, the story went across the whole town; what a MIRACLE! My mother was dubbed a miracle worker.

[REAL LIFE story as told by a former colleague of mine – real names and town withheld].

Miracles like this happen every single day in various parts of the world and spheres of life. If you do not believe in miracles, you may find the story hard to believe, but that does not change the fact that miracles happen. Not only that, but they also happen through the hands of ordinary human beings like you and me. I want to continue the rest of this book by defining the word miracle so that you and I can have a definition to work with.

SO, WHAT IS A MIRACLE?

A miracle, according to the Merriam-Webster Dictionary, is 'an extraordinary event, manifesting divine intervention in human affairs.' In other words, miracles happen when natural laws are suspended.

Do you agree that the story of the little girl and Jyothi was a miracle? It was an extraordinary event without a doubt, given the number of people who had tried to work with the girl; the native doctors that failed, and the several teachers whose attempts had no effect. Divine intervention was necessary, and no, angels did not have to visit the earth; it happened through the hands of a mere mortal like you and me. Human beings are capable of working miracles. Humans have been endowed to suspend natural laws in various spheres of life for unusual things to happen in our world. The miracle of the aeroplane has become mainstream today. The aeroplane suspends the law of gravity and can carry millions of people daily from place to place. Miracles are around us daily.

Human life is also a miracle worth studying. Scientists have found that for a baby to be born, millions of sperm cells compete to fertilise an egg. At the end of the day, only one of those sperms would win the race. When you were born, among millions of other sperms, you emerged as the winner. This is your first miracle. The fact that you are alive, and breathing is a miracle. Scientists have estimated that the probability of you being born is about 1 in 400 trillion chances. That is, you were most likely not supposed to have made it. It is a miracle that you did. It is a miracle that you emerged and were given birth to. You are a walking miracle!

However, this is not the kind of miracle this book is about. Beyond the fact that you were miraculously conceived and birthed, or that you are alive and breathing, this book is about you being a miracle worker. Yes, you read that right. This book is about you performing miracles. Whether you believe it or not, I want you to know that you can work miracles. Just like Jyothi, the teacher that took the young girl in, there is something that you have been divinely entrusted to work miracles with, every single day of your life. The fact that you are alive, and breathing is evidence that God still wants you here to work miracles on His behalf in people's lives.

I love how Jesus puts it,

'I tell you the truth, anyone who believes in me will do the same works I have done, and even greater works, because I am going to be with the Father.' [1]

That scripture is very loaded. What Jesus is simply saying is that for every single miracle that He did while he was here on the earth, you too have the capacity to do the same and even more. But there are criteria, and these are some of the things I will be sharing in this book.

The scripture says '… *anyone who believes….*', it all starts with believing. So many people believe that they are ordinary and that they have no value to offer to their world. As a result, they deny the world of the miracle-working power within them. That is one of the first things I want to leave inside of you as you read this book – **you are not just a walking miracle; you are a miracle worker**.

This means that when you recognise your capacity, and ability to work miracles, you begin to carry yourself differently. The awareness will empower you to see and approach the problems of life differently. This knowledge will also help you to approach your role in people's lives differently. You will realise that you have a major role to play in the grand scheme of things. You are more than just a number in the population of the world. Like Jyothi, you were created to put smiles on people's faces, bring hope to the hopeless, and transform the lives of the people around you because of the value that you carry. Jesus' words in John 14:12 says, '… *anyone who believes…*' So, do you believe that you can work miracles? Do you believe that you are not just a walking miracle, but a miracle worker? Do you believe that you are someone who can work

---

[1] John 14:12 NLT

miracles, not just by your power and might but by the grace and gifts entrusted to you by God?

> *You are not just a walking miracle; you are a miracle worker.*

Again, '…anyone who believes in me will do the same works I have done…' In other words, Jesus is saying the minimum miracles that you have the capacity to do here on earth is exactly what He did. That is the minimum, that is the baseline, and that is the lowest you are allowed to do. Jesus didn't stop there, he also said, 'and even greater works…' This means that God, through you, can express Himself in ways that people will recognise that this is God walking and working among men. This is an intervention of divinity in humanity, and that is exactly what a miracle is.

Do you believe in miracles?

Do you believe in miracles? Or to put it differently, do you believe you can work miracles? My answer is YES! I believe in you, even if you don't believe in yourself. Every human being on this planet has been graced with the gift to work miracles. We all have that power within us. However, that power needs to be activated. My goal is to introduce you to that power and how you can activate it in your life.

Another perspective on miracles

A miracle is a collaboration of divinity with humanity to do something extraordinary. This means God partnering with human beings to do great things here on earth. This is very important because, in every partnership, responsibilities are involved. The reason many people do not tap into their miracle-working abilities is that they are either unaware of this truth or are unwilling to take on the responsibility of partnering with God to do great things on earth.

Jesus went on to say '…because I am going to the father…'[2] which could imply 'I am done doing miracles here on earth by myself. I have given you charge to continue the miracle-working on my behalf.' In other words, 'I have given you the authority, the backing, the influence, and the power.' No wonder the Bible says, 'Now unto him that is able to do exceeding abundantly above all that we ask or think, according to the power that worketh in us.'[3] This means that there is a power in you that works, and that power can work miracles abundantly above what any man can think of.

The Bible also says that '…No eye has seen, no ear has heard, and no mind has imagined what God has prepared for those who love him.'[4] God has prepared these things for you if you would take responsibility and leverage the power and authority He has given you. If you do, you are going to do so much more than Jesus himself did.

You can do greater works than Jesus did on earth. We are still talking about His miracles today. If you will dare to do the miracles that God has given you the capacity and potential to do here on earth, we will continue to talk about your life even after you are gone.

---

[2] John 14:12
[3] Ephesians 3:20 KJV
[4] 1 Corinthians 2:9 NLT

God wants you to work miracles

God wants you to – leverage all that He has given you to partner with Him and be His representative here on earth – do the miracles that He wants to do here. Every time someone comes to you with a problem, you realise that there is a power inside of you, and you activate that power through your partnership with God. God is looking for men and women in various spheres of life who will, every single day, wake up and be that agent of transformation in our world, be it in politics, science, media, education, arts, or entertainment. Even in the spiritual realm, God is looking for men and women, like Habakkuk, who will climb up to their watchtowers and stand at their guard posts to avail and prevail on behalf of their nations and generations.

History has a record of various men and women who stood in the gap in their generations to cause a change. Talk about **Nelson Mandela**; the miracle of South Africa we still talk about today because he partnered with God to bring freedom to his people. Talk about the **Wright Brothers** who dedicated their lives to flying a plane despite the law of gravity; the miracle of flying came about today because they stayed through to their cause. Talk about the miracle of arts and paintings, we sure must mention the likes of **Pablo Picasso** and **Michael Angelo**. What about music? You would agree with me that there are very few people that command such prowess and authority as **Beethoven and Mozart**. These were walking miracles in their lifetime and even in death, they are still changing lives.

The question is, what miracle will you be remembered for? You already have the ability and authority. Remember that Jesus said, 'I am going to my father.' I always say that God created trees, but He didn't create chairs. God created cotton but He didn't create jeans or suits. God left all of that for us to create them. These are the miracles that we, as human beings, are going to be remembered for. The power is already within you, so, what miracles are you going to be remembered for?

LIFE'S GREATEST MIRACLE

The miracle of a changed life

I believe that the greatest miracle is the miracle of a changed life. Jesus did many miracles while on earth. The record in the scriptures says He worked about thirty-seven or thirty-eight miracles. We also heard that he healed 'many' which means those who were healed were not counted. There were times Jesus did miracles for a whole day. Jesus did tonnes of miracles but the greatest miracle, which was Jesus' purpose, was to bring salvation to man.

This tells us that the greatest miracle on earth is the miracle of a changed life. Just like Jyothi in the story I shared in the introduction, she came in and changed everything about that little girl that everyone had given up on. The greatest miracle is not when the blind see. While that is awesome, it is not the greatest miracle. It is also not when someone recovers from cancer, the greatest miracle is when someone's life is completely changed, and they are transformed to think and behave differently. This is the essence of the gospel Jesus came to preach.

Jesus' message of 'Repent for the kingdom of heaven is at hand' was misunderstood during his time, and till today, that misunderstanding still exists. People have associated repentance with penance and guilt, whereas that was not what Jesus preached. Repent in the original Greek translation refers to 'transformation of the heart' or simply put, 'transformational thinking.' Jesus was simply saying,

God's kingdom requires a different way of thinking. It requires a changed heart – one that aligns with God's way of thinking.

Following Jesus' essence here on earth, I believe we are commissioned to do the very same thing Jesus did and preach here on earth in the various spheres of life which we have been sent or called into. Since man fell into sin, God has been busy with the change of man's life. The change of a man's heart and thinking is a very tough job.

Don't copy the behaviour and customs of this world, <u>but let God transform you into a new person by changing the way you think</u>. Then you will learn to know God's will for you, which is good and pleasing and perfect.[5]

A miracle is when someone's way of thinking completely changes, and that is why it is the toughest job in the world. People love to see change but when the change is about them, they run away. But if we are going to transform our world, the change must begin with us. Every miracle starts with the miracle worker. For us to do miracles on earth, we must first experience the miracle of a changed life.

Dear reader, I hope that you have experienced this miracle I'm referring to and that you are born again because the process of working miracles begins with this. Put differently, the miracle must begin with you, your life must first change for you to be able to change other people's lives because you cannot give what you don't have. I have come to realise that what changes other people is the testimony of your own changed life. For instance, if people who knew you before see you again in a transformed state,

---

[5] Romans 12:2 NLT (Emphasis Added)

this is substantial evidence for them to believe whatever you have to say about a changed life.

The formula for a miracle (divinity and humanity working in collaboration)

What is the formula for changing a man's life? What is the formula for bringing divine intervention into a man's experience? I believe that formula is divinity plus humanity in partnership. Anytime God wants to interfere in the affairs of men, He will need a man. God is seeking a man in every generation to carry out what He wants to do on earth. I always like to say it like this that, God is looking for a man who will begin on earth what He has already completed in heaven. If you look all through the scriptures, you will find out that for a miracle to happen, man and God always must work in tandem.

It is almost impossible in our earthly realm for God to come down to do anything by Himself. God will often come down in the form of a man. Even for the greatest miracle in life right now which is salvation, God had to come in the form of man. This tells us that many of the miracles God will do in our generation have to come by you and I working in tandem with God. If you don't work in tandem with God, you will be denying your generation the miracles that you are supposed to do.

> *God is looking for a man who will begin on earth what He has already completed in heaven*

God asked Moses in the Bible, 'What is in your hand?' and Moses said, 'A rod' and that was the rod God used to deliver a nation from hundreds of years of slavery. The prophet Elisha asked that widow, 'What is in your house?'[6] and the widow said, 'Nothing but a jar of oil' and that jar of oil multiplied and delivered the widow and her family from poverty. It reminds me also of the widow of Zarephath whom God sent Elijah to meet. She only had a morsel of bread that she and her son would eat and die, but that was what God used. Worthy of remembrance is the young boy who only had five loaves of bread and two fishes that fed five thousand people.

Every miracle has encoded in it the responsibility of man and the conditions that he must fulfil. Anytime God and man work together, miracles happen. If we work with divinity in tandem, we create a platform for miracles to happen. However, we must fulfil a condition for the miracle to happen. Maybe it is in putting your rod down for it to turn into a snake, or maybe it is preparing your last morsel of bread that you think you and your son will eat and die but allowing God to make it greater. Maybe it is that jar of oil that you have in your hands, and you must borrow vessels to pour it into and it never runs out.

You have a part to play to work miracles or see God's intervention in every situation. God's part in every miracle is certain, that is because everything that is playing out to God is past tense to Him. Everything we are experiencing right now was already done in God's sight. God doesn't begin what He has not completed. Hence, we call Him Alpha and Omega – the beginning and the end. He knows

---

[6] 2 kings 4

the end from the beginning. This is the reason why God is always faithful. He is always faithful because He is not confused by whatever humans do. He is faithful because He has already done His part. You must do your part by taking the responsibility to fulfil the conditions for that miracle to happen. We see that all through the scriptures, including some of the examples that I have shared earlier.

Every time you trust God for a miracle, you must look for the condition to fulfil and your responsibility - the part you must play.

The question god is always asking

God is always looking for a man who will fulfil that responsibility, so the question He is always asking in every generation including our current generation, which He is asking you right now is, *'Whom shall I send?'*

God has been asking that question from the very foundation of the earth and He is still asking today. *'Also I heard the voice of the Lord, saying, whom shall I send, and who will go for us? Then said I, here am I; send me.* [7] Anytime there is a response of humanity to divinity's 'whom shall I send', a miracle is about to break forth. When the manifestation of the sons of men is about to happen, the glory of God is about to be seen in its full weight and expression.

In every single generation, God is always looking for men to commission and people that will co-create with Him. God is looking for those who will do significant and mighty things because, through them, He will express Himself such that humanity will see God in man. We saw

---

[7] Isaiah 6:8 KJV

that through Jesus Christ, the Apostle Paul, and the lives of various mighty men and women in the Bible. When God wanted to deliver Israel from the oppression of Goliath, who was intimidating and threatening the entire host of Israel for forty days and forty nights, God probably looked through the army and couldn't find anybody, so He had to get a 17-year-old boy called David, who was abandoned in the bush to be killed by lions and bears, untrained in the army but was brave and ready to partner with God.

This young boy who was sent to deliver lunch saw how intimidated the armies of Israel were, gnashing their teeth because of Goliath. He was so irritated. He asked, 'What would be given to the man who kills this uncircumcised Philistine?' He was so bold because he had been working with God in the secret place. He had been working in tandem with God to experience miracles of killing the lion and the bear and he couldn't wait to show Goliath his curriculum vitae. He told Goliath, '*I have killed the lions and the bears that wanted to attack my father's sheep and I would do the same to you.*'[8]

That can only come from a man who has been working with God in tandem in the secret place. I often say that greatness is doing excellently in public what you have been doing in secret. David believed that because God could kill the lion and the bear through him, then a human being like himself won't be an exception. He knew precisely what he was doing; he didn't come in his name but in the name of the King of kings and the Lord of lords. God is always looking for a man in every generation. Will you be that

---

[8] 1 Samuel 17

man? Will you be that woman? Sometimes, God would ask 'Whom shall I send?' and nobody would be there.

'And I sought for a man among them, that should make up the hedge, and stand in the gap before me for the land, that I should not destroy it: but I found none.'[9]

This reminds me of the story of Lot, when God wanted to destroy Sodom and Gomorrah, and Abraham was interceding on their behalf. He had to be asking, Lord , if you find 30, 20, or 10 because it was so hard to find a man who would stand in the gap. I love Isaiah's response to God's call. He said, 'Here am I, send me.'[10]

Anytime humanity responds to God's call, a miracle is about to break forth in the earth's realm. This is one key to working miracles. If you would decide right now that you would be God's expression in our generation and the generations to come, you would witness miracles wrought by your hands. Also, you would witness God express Himself through you in ways that you would not have been able to imagine because eyes have not seen, ears have not heard, neither has it been in the hearts of man, the plans of God.

Do not allow yourself to be seduced by everything else in the world; the rat race, competition, wealth, and luxury. You are an embodiment of God's call. Your needs would leave you empty and void but if you respond to God's need for a man in our generation, it will give your life meaning, significance, influence, and impact more than you have ever seen before. Like Isaiah, your answer must be 'Here I am, send me.'

---

[9] Ezekiel 22:30 KJV
[10] Isaiah 6:8

Why work miracles?

1. To bring glory to God

The Greek word for glory is the word 'doxa' which means 'full weight of, or full expression of.' In other words, 'glory' is God putting Himself on display through man. The glory of God is the full nature of God on display and God wants to display His full nature through you. Therefore, you must work miracles.

People must see you and see the glory of God in and through you. Just as the glory of God covered the earth as water covers the sea, you must be that expression of the Glory of God.

2. To expand the Kingdom here on earth

There is no way you would tell people you are a child of God if you cannot work miracles by your hand, or if God cannot do something extraordinary by your hand. Jesus said, 'If they do not see signs and wonders, they would not believe.' If you must bring people into the kingdom of God, if you must depopulate hell and populate heaven, then you must work miracles and do greater works than Jesus did.

3. To shine as light

'Arise, shine; For your light has come! And the glory of the Lord is risen upon you.'[11]

The word for light in the text above means 'to bring order.' This means that when a man rises, shines and he does what God has called him to do, he brings order. All

---

[11] Isaiah 60:1 NKJV

the places that the devil has brought disorder to, you would just come there and there will be order. To bring order is to allow God to express Himself through you.

4. To be an expression of God to the world

'For the earnest expectation of the creature waiteth for the manifestation of the sons of God.'[12]

That word translated as manifestation in that verse is the word 'apokalupsis.' It means the revelation, light that brings order. It is talking about the sons of God, that is you reading this right now; God wants to use you and the creation is awaiting your manifestation.

5. We have been given as a mandate

We have been given the authority to work miracles. Jesus said, '…*All authority in heaven and earth has been given to me, therefore go into the world…*'[13] This means that you have been commissioned and you have the backing of divinity to work miracles. You have authority here on earth to work miracles.

---

[12] Romans 8:9 KJV
[13] Matthew 28:19-20 Paraphrased

CHAPTER TWO

THERE ARE PROBLEMS YOU WERE BORN TO SOLVE

Before there can be a miracle, there must be a problem. Problems are the breakfast of champions. Great people who have discovered their greatness don't run away from problems. They run towards the problems that they were born to solve because if there are no problems, there will be no need for solution carriers. Darkness necessitates the essence of light. The Bible says when light shines, darkness cannot comprehend it.

This means that your presence here on earth is necessary because of the problems that sin has brought into the world. In fact, problems reveal the miracle-working power that you carry. When next you see a problem around you, don't be one of those people who become afraid and chicken out or run away like the armies of Israel before Goliath. Be that person that stands boldly in the face of Goliath and says, '*Who is this uncircumcised Philistine defiling the armies of the living God?*' Be that person who would stand and lead other people in the face of a crisis.

As I said in my book, *Purpose in Crisis*, 'Crisis is a call to leadership.' It is your call to emerge as a leader. Every problem or crisis is calling out for something within you and that thing is already there. That thing has already been deposited inside you before you were born. It was part of your make-up, part of your essence. God puts a solution inside of you and that is the reason for the crisis around you or that you're experiencing. Therefore, you must never run away from problems. Any time you hear someone complaining about their lack of freedom, or someone being oppressed around you, there is a likelihood that their problem is calling out for the solutions inside of you. Don't back out. Don't be of those who pull back, instead, respond to the calling on your inside by faith.

Now, I recognise that we were not called to solve all problems, so it is important to know the problems to focus on. Let me share with you ten keys to help you identify the problems you were born to solve.

> *Every problem or crisis is calling out for something within you and that thing is already there*

How to discover the problems you were born to solve

1. What problems or issues in the world make me legitimately angry?

People can be illegitimately angry. That is the kind of anger the Bible admonishes us against and that is not the kind of anger I want to talk about. I am talking about the problems in our world that make you want to jump up and do something, or put together a team to solve them, or raise funds to solve.

In the scriptures, Moses was angry when he saw an Egyptian maltreating a Hebrew man. There was something on his inside that got him so angry that he had to kill the Egyptian. I am not asking you to go and kill someone but please, get the point. There is something that makes you legitimately angry to solve a particular problem. You must not neglect that anger. You must take the problem personally even if other people around you do not feel the same way. Everyone around you might wonder why it affects or bothers you the way it does. The reason it affects you so much is because there is something on your inside that is calling out to solve that problem. Miracles await you if you answer the call.

2. What issue or problem in the world saddens my heart?

What is that thing that every time you experience it or see someone experiencing it, gets you sad? More like you break down in tears not just in sympathy or pity but the fact that you feel you could do something about it.

I remember the story of a friend who would get saddened by many women in the hospital who don't have sanitary pads and all the necessary resources needed to take care of their children after delivery because of poverty. Because of that sadness, she had to start doing something about it with her own money. Today, people are donating millions of dollars to her to solve that problem because she decided to become the miracle worker in that case.

So, what problem saddens your heart?

3. What will bring me my greatest fulfilment?

Many of us know the answer to this question and if you do, I want to challenge you to live your life going after your answer. What is the problem that when you solve will give you the greatest fulfilment? For me, it is helping people discover their purpose. Every single time I stand on the podium to speak or sit with people one-on-one or in groups to coach them, and I am helping them discover their purpose, you need to come and see me after I am done. I am full of energy. I feel like I don't need to eat anything else because I am satisfied. That is why I want to do it every single day. This is a sign of fulfilment. Helping people discover their life's purpose is my force field of miracles.

4. What am I truly passionate about?

Passion speaks about fire and hunger! If purpose is the vehicle, passion is the fuel. What problems stirs up a hunger or fire in you to resolve? For me, it is helping people discover their purpose. That is what I am always passionate about. Every single time, it is what I am talking about. Don't even get me started talking about purpose. We could be there for days, and I will not get tired. If you listen to me speak, either live or via my podcast or YouTube channel, you will notice that when I start speaking about purpose, I may start slowly but as it goes on, I become so full of energy and zeal that I can't seem to control because purpose is my passion. It is a topic that stirs up the fire in my bones, and I can't curtail my energy.

You too have something that you are so energetic about and can't curtail your passion for it. I am not talking about other passions like things you are not called to do. For instance, I am very passionate about football, but I am not called to be a footballer. No matter the amount of time I spend playing, watching, or analysing football, it would not bring any solution to the world because I am not great at it. But when it comes to the subject of purpose, you would find me there and that is where I can bring solutions to the world. 'What am I truly passionate about?' is a very powerful question.

5.   What do I constantly imagine or see myself doing?

While I was a teenager, every time I tried to envisage the next ten or twenty years of my life, I would always see myself in front of a large audience speaking. In my myopic mind, I thought I was going to become a teacher; I thought the vision was to become a professor. What I did not know was that God was showing me that I was going to become a change agent in my world, that I was going to be a people builder. I didn't know at that time, but every time I closed my eyes that was what I saw.

Every time you imagine your future self, what do you see? Do you see yourself in front of a large audience like me, do you see yourself owning a large corporation? What you see is often a pointer to the miracle that you are destined to work on the surface of the earth.

6.   How do I want to serve humanity?

'For David, after he had served his own generation by the will of God, fell asleep, was buried with his fathers, and saw corruption'[14]

There must be a hunger to serve your generation in you and that hunger is your call to work miracles. To work miracles, you must address that hunger to serve your generation and serve passionately. What is that area of life you would give your all, come rain or shine?

---

[14] Acts 13:36 NKJV

7. What solutions are present in my heart and mind?

As I said earlier on, where there is a nagging problem that you take personally, there is also a nagging solution impressed upon your heart to give to the world. For some people, it is the solution to produce clothes for people, while for others, it is a solution to produce good quality music. They have seen how bad music keeps multiplying in our world today and they just want to address that by solving the problem. You would become a miracle worker by bringing that solution to that area or sphere of life.

8. What would I do for no money or other compensation?

Peter and John were going to the temple at the hour of prayer and they saw this man who had been lame since he was born.[15] The Bible says the man looked at them expecting to receive something (money) from them but Peter and John didn't have the money he was looking for, so they looked him in the eyes and said, '*Silver and gold we don't have, but that which we have...*' Stop worrying about what you don't have. God does not need what you don't have. Pay attention to what you have, instead. That is the one God is more interested in using if you would surrender it to Him.

Peter and John said, '*That which we have, we give to you, in the name of Jesus rise up and walk*' and that was how they were able to work a miracle.

What would you do for no compensation or money? Even though, later, you will be duly compensated for the

---

[15] Acts 3

solutions you bring to people's lives and society, you must be willing to do it now for no compensation.

9. What would I do if I know I won't fail?

Every human being on the surface of the earth can do one thing with a relatively high degree of accuracy and not fail in it. When they perform that act, it is more as if it is God doing it through them. I am going to tell you more about that in another chapter. In my book, *Purpose in Crisis*, I talked about 'The Dimension of God in you.' It is a personal revelation God gave me and I will tell you more about it.

When you find that dimension of God in you, it is impossible for you to fail. When you can't fail, that is you working miracles.

10. What activity connects me with God the most?

Anytime a man finds the solution that they carry, it connects them to God in the most unique ways possible. Because it is the expression of God through you, it is that joint that connects you and God and makes you both one channel. It connects you with God and connects other people to God through you.

These are the ten questions you need to answer, if you can answer these ten questions and all your answers are sticking around one area or maybe two or three, I want you to write them down because those are the areas that you are supposed to focus your entire time and energy on, pouring your life inside of them. That is how you can discover the miracles that you are born to solve.

You must watch out for the problems yelling out your name

You must also watch out for the problems that are yelling your name. In my book, *Purpose in Crisis*, I talked about how certain problems are yelling your name. I don't know what your name is, but my name is Samuel, and every time I find someone who hasn't found their purpose, who seems like they are living a meaningless life without impact and influence, there is something that is yelling my name. Before I know it, I want to meet with the person over a cup of coffee or virtually on Zoom. Sometimes, I would have given them an appointment almost without giving it too much thought. I always want to talk to them. There is always that desire and many times, I have to hold myself back either as a caution or courtesy. In my heart, I just want to jump up and solve the problem because it seems to be yelling my name.

In the story of David and Goliath, which is one of my favourite stories in the Bible, David could not bear to see Goliath parading himself and releasing threats before the armies of Israel. He just couldn't bear it because the problem was yelling out his name. It reminds me of how African parents would call their children, 'David, oooh!' It seemed like the oppression of the children of Israel was yelling, 'David, oooh!' David said, *'I know I came to deliver lunch, but can I ask what would be given to the person that kills this guy?' The motive behind that question is 'There is something I cannot bear, something is calling out my name about this problem. I want to kill this guy. I have the solution to this problem.'* When his brothers heard that he was asking what would be given to the man who killed Goliath, they said, 'You have come again,' but David was not deterred.

You must know that there is a problem calling out your name, and every time you stand to solve that problem, your friends and family might say 'You have come again.' Whenever there is a nagging desire within you to work a miracle, know that it is the solution inside of you calling out your name. My next piece of advice to you is to run after that problem and devote your life to it. Even if no one will pay you for it yet, even if it does not put food on the table yet, devote your life to it. Begin to solve that problem right now with whatever it is you have, don't worry about what you don't have. David went after Goliath with a slingshot. The slingshot was what he had, and it was his master tool for killing all the dangerous animals that had crossed his path before his encounter with Goliath.

Saul, the king, did not want David to face Goliath with just a slingshot, so he gave him his sword and armour but by the time David was dressed up in them, they weighed him down. He struggled, so he protested. He refused to wear them, and he went with what he had. He went with the passion that was burning on his inside. With that slingshot and five stones, David killed Goliath. Thousands of years later, the story is still relevant on our lips. The miracle is still being told!

Be that person, like Esther, who would go before the king despite all the hindrances. Say to yourself, 'If I perish, I perish but I am going after this problem.' Be like Nehemiah who had a good job in the palace being the king's cupbearer but decided that he was going to rebuild the walls of Jerusalem because the problem was yelling out his name and he was not ready to back down on his generation.

The miracle you were born to wrought is yelling out your name every single day. You wake up and you hear that problem calling your name, you want to sleep and it's calling your name. It keeps you up at night and wakes you up in the morning. Stop looking at every other place for your purpose, this is the reason you were born. Your time has come to grace your valley of Elah. Get your slingshot and five stones ready, go to that battle in the name of the Lord as David did, and bring down the head of your Goliath.

> *The miracle you were born to wrought is yelling out your name every single day*

When you serve your generation like David did, you work miracles. When you answer the call of that problem that is yelling your name, you are answering your calling. When you answer your call, God will cause everything concerning you to work perfectly.

YOU'RE CARRYING SOMETHING

You're carrying something

What you are carrying is the source of the miracle that the world needs. In other words, what you carry on the inside of you is the solution to some of the chronic issues and problems of our world. It would be a tragedy to live life as though you are not carrying anything. You cannot afford to live life as if you don't matter or your life doesn't count. Your life counts because you carry the solution to a problem that the world is afflicted with.

This reminds me of something that happened where I used to work a few years ago. There was a particular problem in the I.T. unit of that organisation and I saw everybody running helter-skelter trying to solve the problem. And the whole place was in chaos as a result. Interestingly, they were asking everyone in the room, but no one asked me. I was the only African in the room, while there were other people of colour. At a point, I was beginning to believe it must be because of my skin colour – perhaps I had been stereotyped as very unlikely to carry the solution to a problem that others could not solve. They felt I wouldn't have the answers.

Interestingly, I came across the same problem some days earlier and I was so determined to solve it. I even stayed extra time at work to solve the problem and I saw to it that I had it solved. I ended up solving it on the eve of the chaotic day at work. No one knew that I had encountered and solved the problem earlier because I hadn't mentioned it to anyone.

When I noticed that they were uneasy, I asked someone 'What's the problem?' Just like David had to ask when he got to the valley of Elah where Goliath was oppressing the Israelites. The person I asked said, 'It's this particular bug that no one seems to have a solution to.' I said to him, 'I know the solution. I encountered it some days earlier and worked hard to resolve it.' He couldn't believe his ears. He took me to one of the Team Leaders and within fifteen minutes, I was able to resolve it, and everyone saw me in a different light from that day going forward.

The point I am trying to make is; don't ever look down on yourself that you are insignificant. Don't ever think that you have nothing to show for your existence. Don't ever believe that you are not carrying something that the world needs. The world needs you. That is the title of one of my books, *THE WORLD NEEDS YOU: Life-changing Secrets to Becoming a Person of Value*. I shared in that book that everyone is carrying something of value on the inside. You are carrying something so valuable, it's the miracle that this world needs.

I shared a story earlier that I want to go back to to expatiate this point. Peter and John were going to the temple at the hour of prayer, and they met a man who had been lame from his birth at the gate of the temple called The Beautiful Gate. The man was always there every single day and his problem remained with him. His problem might have existed long before Peter and John were born. And probably, that was not the first time they were seeing him. But on that day, something called forth for the solution that Peter and John were carrying to perform the miracle that would go on to change the man's life. While the man was expecting them to give him money, what they gave him was much more powerful.

'Peter looked straight at him, as did John. Then Peter said, "Look at us!" So, the man gave them his attention, expecting to get something from them. Then Peter said, "Silver or gold I do not have, but what I do have I give you. In the name of Jesus Christ of Nazareth, walk." Taking him by the right hand, he helped him up, and instantly the man's feet and ankles became strong.'[16]

You might be reading this, and people think that you don't have anything they need or will ever need, because you don't look like it, don't let that deter you. You might not have the money that they think they need but what they really need is what you have. Some people think they need money but what they need is way more than money, and you could be carrying their miracle on your inside. You must know how to recognise that miracle inside of you so that you can know how to address their needs. There is a difference between what people want and what they really need. Most times, people don't ask for what they need. Peter and John recognised the man had a bigger need than he was asking for daily, so they didn't give the man money like other people were doing. They realised if they gave him money, he would continue to stay at that gate asking people for money. But the miracle inside of Peter and John was able to liberate that man from his shackles and the oppression holding him down. He was freed to live fully!

____

[16] Acts 3:4-7 NIV

The miracle you are carrying right now can liberate people and set them free from long-standing problems, problems that have perhaps been around before you were born. You will be able to do all of that if you would only recognise that you are carrying a miracle inside of you.

'Then Peter said, "**Silver or gold I do not have, but what I do have** I give you. In the name of Jesus Christ of Nazareth, walk.'[17]

Again, it is not about what you don't have, it's about what you have. Stop looking at other people who have other luxurious things that you don't have. Many times, in life, we compare what we have with what other people have and immediately discount what we have. If you do that, you are going to be like the man who received one talent and went to bury it.[18] That is not what God needs from you. God wants you to realise that whatever you have is what the world needs and it has the potential to birth miracles. You cannot afford to take it for granted. The miracle on our inside is bigger than silver and gold. What you are carrying is not what the world wants but what the world needs.

I need to point this out to you, your miracle cannot happen outside of God, your miracle can only happen in God. If you live like everybody else without acknowledging God, your life would be ordinary but if you want to have a lasting impact that would be beyond your generation, which is what I call transgenerational influence like the miracle that Peter and John did in Acts 3 which we are still

---

[17] Acts 3:6 NIV
[18] Matthew 25:24-25

talking about today, thousands of years after, you must acknowledge God.

You would notice that all the examples I have been giving from the start of this book have been transgenerational miracles. You carry the same power to work miracles and solve problems that have existed even before your parents were born. Stop comparing yourself with other people. It is not about what you don't have. It is about what you have, and you must value what you have for you to work miracles with it.

Only you can do what you have been called to do. This is why you cannot afford not to do what you have been called to do. If you refuse to use what you are carrying, you are going to deny generations of the miracles inside you. There are many generational thieves in our world today, who keep denying generations of what they are carrying.

That book that God has asked you to write is the miracle that the world is waiting for. That business that God has asked you to start is the miracle that generations are waiting for. That speaking that God has asked you to do is the miracle the world is waiting for. You keep thinking that you don't have anything to offer, what you don't know is that what you carry is what the world needs, so don't despise it, or ignore it.

The solutions you bring into people's lives: you have these solutions and must pass them on to others

1. Light

You do not just bring light to darkness; you are the light of the world[19] No wonder the Bible says, 'And the light shines in the darkness, and the darkness did not comprehend it.'[20] The Bible also says, 'Arise, shine; For your light has come! And the glory of the Lord is risen upon you.'[21]

Anywhere you see light, you see glory. Anywhere you see light, darkness disappears, and this is the solution you bring into people's lives. Some people have been weeping but when you show up suddenly, they experience the light of God. Hear how the Bible puts it, *The people walking in darkness have seen a great light; on those living in the land of deep darkness a light has dawned*[22]

I remember there was a time a lady came to me that she wanted to commit suicide and by the time we were done with a 90-minutes session of giving her clarity and talking to her, with the help of God, light came, and darkness disappeared. She felt a new sense of hope. Light shone into the room and her life.

2. Order amid Chaos

Our world has a lot of chaos going on now. Just like the story I shared with you earlier in this chapter, everyone in the office was in a state of chaos but as soon as I stepped into the situation, suddenly everyone could go back to their

---

[19] Matthew 5:14
[20] John 1:5 NKJV
[21] Isaiah 60:1 NKJV
[22] Isaiah 9:2 NIV

work. Order was restored because someone with the solution was in the room.

This is literally what God has called you to do in our world. Wherever there is chaos, you show up with the solution that you have on your inside and there is order.

3. Freedom from Oppression

There are so many people in our world who are oppressed by the devil, oppressed by sickness, oppressed by poverty, or oppressed by ignorance.

I believe that the greatest form of oppression is ignorance. When a man has knowledge of who he is and the purpose of God for his life, suddenly, he is set free. This is what I wake up to do every morning to see someone discover their purpose and be free from the oppression of ignorance of their purpose.

The solution you are carrying will give people freedom from every oppression in their lives.

4. Productivity and Effectiveness

Many people are just going around in circles. They are not productive and have no results to show for their lives and existence. Once you show up to offer the solution of clarity, it brings effectiveness. You can remove the barriers and roadblocks that are holding them back from doing what God has called them to do. You help them remove their excuses or fears and become productive with results to show for it.

5. Safety and Protection

So many people are endangered in our world today; endangered by sickness, endangered by a false sense of identity and suddenly you come into the scene, and you provide safety and protection.

This brings me to the story of when the disciples of Jesus were travelling in a boat and there was a massive storm. Jesus was sleeping and the disciples came to him saying, 'Lord, careth not thou that we perish?' and Jesus said, 'Peace be still' and the storm calmed and there was safety.

The Apostle Paul was also in a shipwreck, and he told those who were with him that 'We are not going to die, God has spoken to me that I am going to stand before the King today. So don't worry guys, this shipwreck is not going to affect anything. If you stay on the boat, you are safe.' The men did, and they were safe.

6. Preservation

Preservation speaks about legacy; it speaks about transgenerational impacts and influence. You bring solutions to people that will be able to preserve their lives from generation to generation. When you are able to bring out what God has put in your inside, people are preserved. A good example is that young boy with five loaves and two fishes who was able to preserve the lives of 5000 men, apart from women and children[23].

7. Kingdom Expansion

Whenever you bring the solution God has put inside of you out to serve the world, what happens is that there is Kingdom expansion. God will use you to depopulate hell

---

[23] Matthew 14:21

and populate heaven. There is no greater ministry than the desire to expand God's kingdom.

Jesus gave us a blueprint that is life changing. He said, 'Seek the (expansion of) Kingdom of God above all else, and live righteously, and he will give you everything you need.'24 God has deposited solutions inside you that will birth influence. When you then have this influence and people are following you, you will point them to the Kingdom of God.

8. Promotion

Some people are stuck in the same place for years and don't know what to do, just like that man who was stuck at the Beautiful Gate, every single day, asking for alms. As soon as Peter and John worked that miracle, that man would no longer be found at that gate. Record has it that the man began to leap and walk and jump and was shouting everywhere praising God. He was promoted from sitting at the Beautiful Gate to running around in freedom and praising God.

When you allow God to use what you carry, many who are stuck or stagnant will begin to receive their promotion. They will become unstuck and free to also live their purpose.

9. A Sense of Purpose and Meaning

This is my testimony; anytime people meet me or come to our school - School of Purpose and Influence (SPIN) - or they book a clarity or coaching session with me, there is a renewed sense of purpose or hope. This is the solution I

---

[24] Matthew 6:33 NLT (Emphasis Mine)

bring to my world, and this is the miracle I am working in my generation and the ones to come. Not only do the people who encounter me go away with a renewed sense of meaning and purpose, but I also experience it too. The more I use what God has put inside of me as solutions to the problems of others, the more fulfilled and meaningful I feel.

10. The Knowledge of the Glory of God

'For the earth will be filled with the knowledge of the glory of the Lord as the waters cover the sea'[25]

Every time you work the miracles that God has ordained you to work, you are spreading the knowledge of the glory of God across the earth. 'Glory' means full expression. Every time you work miracles, people see through you the full expression of God. They can't see God physically, but they are able to experience who He is through you. Jesus made a statement that relays this well when He said, 'Anyone who has seen Me has seen the Father.'[26]

> *Every time you work the miracles that God has ordained you to work, you are spreading the knowledge of the glory of God across the earth*

11. Sense of Identity

We live in a world where people do not know who they really are. They wake up every day trying to be everyone else but themselves. They have been sold all kinds of lies,

---

[25] Habakkuk 2:14 NIV
[26] John 14:9 AMP

from the Evolution Theory to Astrology. This is the source of people living inauthentic lives and if they continue to live a lie, they cannot truly become all that God has created them to be. One of the benefits of the solutions God has put on your inside is to help people reconnect to the truth about who they really are in God. And when they know this truth, the truth sets them free!

12. Maximising Potential

One of the miracles you work in the world is to help people maximise their potential and realise that they can do more, be more, and be everything God has created them to be. You can help point them to the untapped potential within them. You can help them rob the grave of their potential. Whatever sphere of influence God has called you into, let people realise that they have something on their inside anytime they encounter you. People who just sit by watching you do what God has called you to do, receive inspiration for theirs. This is why you cannot lay low or give excuses about shining as light in the world. You are carrying something the world needs.

CHAPTER FOUR

THE DIMENSION OF GOD IN YOU

The key to working miracles is the dimension

'And the LORD God formed man of the dust of the ground and breathed into his nostrils the breath of life; and man became a living soul'[27]

I remember reading that scripture some years ago during my quiet time and I asked God some questions about what it really meant. I asked God if He put His entire self into man and I felt God said, 'No, I didn't put all of myself inside of man. I put a dimension or an atom of myself inside of every man.'

Then I went on to do some study and I realised that the Hebrew word translated as '*breath*' in that scripture is the word *'neshâmâh' and it means inspiration*. That means when God breathed into man, God inspired man. God put inspiration inside of a man. That means that the breath of God inside of man inspires man in an area of life. In other words, man has been inspired to do something on earth exactly the way God would do it.

When I asked God that question during my quiet time, God continued, 'If I put my entire self into man, man would become GOD and that is against my nature.' As a result of the dimension of God that we all carry in our inside, we are gods but not GOD. This is so powerful because it allows you to realise that the dimension of God

---

[27] Genesis 2:7 KJV

on your inside is the key to your dominion in life. In other words, there is an area of life, a sphere of life, that you have been given authority to rule and dominate in and you have also been given unparalleled inspiration by God to do it.

The word *'neshâmâh' also* means spirit. The breath of God is the Spirit of God. There is the Spirit of God inside of you and when you know this, this scripture will make so much sense to you, *'But there is a spirit in man, And the breath of the Almighty gives him understanding.*[28]

The inspiration of God in your life gives you understanding in an area of life. In other words, there is a sphere of life where you possess an innate and uncommon understanding. You may not be aware of it now, but that does not mean it is not true. I often tell people that there is an area of life where they can perform at the level of GOD. Often, it could be in one area or two areas and it is often not a lot. A person who has found the dimension of God on their inside, everything they do within the confines of that dimension, is like they are working miracles. It is supernatural. It is the Spirit of God at work that has given them an uncommon understanding so deep that when they act, it is as if God Himself is functioning in that realm. The dimension of God on your inside is the expression of God through you. When you become conscious of this gift, in whatever sphere of life you are called into, you will never compete with anybody.

Again, it is an area of life where you carry the Spirit and grace of God to do and undo - to command things and exercise dominion. This is an expression of the authority God has given to you in that sphere. For some people, it is

---

[28] Job 32:8 NKJV

in fashion, for others it is cooking, writing, or serving in the army. They just do it in a way that nobody else can. There is something about these people that is exceptional and unparalleled.

> *The inspiration of God in your life gives you understanding in an area of life*

This reminds me of a period I was working in an industry some years ago. There was this guy who was so good at computers. Whenever any challenging situation arose, if you took it to him, it was sorted. The way the guy operated the computer was so exceptional. He was so knowledgeable and insightful.

I also remember some time ago; I was preaching somewhere, and I had to play a tape of Steve Jobs giving a speech when the first iPhone came out. I played that video to my audience, and I asked them what they noticed. Some said they noticed he was confident, some said he was very knowledgeable, and so on. I asked them if they noticed that they were watching a master, not just at his craft but in his domain; a king in his territory. The guy was speaking with so much authority that it looked like he was prophesying. He was talking about what we were going to see with the phone in the next ten or twenty years. He was right because we are seeing most of those things he said right now. The guy was not even a child of God but remember, 'There is a spirit in man, the breath of the Almighty that gives him understanding.' It does not matter whether the man is born again or not. This is why as a child of God, you have a greater advantage.

May I let you know that every single man on the face of the earth, 8 billion of us, has the Spirit (inspiration) of God on their inside and He doesn't take it back? The Bible says, 'The gifts of God are irrevocable.'[29] This is why every single human being on the surface of the earth longs for a connection with God. And whenever there is no connection with God, there is an emptiness, a void, and meaninglessness that chases you down because the spirit that is inside of you wants to connect with God in order for you to experience the dimension of God on your inside. It's like a plug that hasn't found the right socket. Despite the potential of the plug, without the right socket, there is a void, a sense of meaninglessness or uselessness. No matter what you could do with that dimension of God in you, if you use it for another purpose rather than for what it was given, you are never going to be successful in the eyes of God.

The source of the miracle you are born to do here on earth is that dimension of God on your inside. You must discover it, develop it, and you must deploy it to serve your generation and the Kingdom of God. If you don't, you will live and die ordinary. You must respond to God through the expression of the Spirit of God on your inside. Your miracle domain is rooted in that dimension of God on your inside.

Some scriptural illustrations

'There are different kinds of spiritual gifts, but the same Spirit is the source of them all.'[30]

---

[29] Romans 11:29
[30] 1 Corinthians 12:4 NLT

Every one of us has different gifts, different dimensions of God on our inside but they all come from the same Spirit. No wonder Peter and John said at that Beautiful Gate that they don't have silver and gold but what they have they gave. That is an invoking of the Spirit of God inside of them to heal that man.

'The Spirit of the Lord came powerfully upon him so that he tore the lion apart with his bare hands as he might have torn a young goat. But he told neither his father nor his mother what he had done.'[31]

'Then the Lord spoke to Moses, saying: "See, I have called by name Bezalel the son of Uri, the son of Hur, of the tribe of Judah. And I have filled him with the Spirit of God, in wisdom, in understanding, in knowledge, and in all manner of workmanship, to design artistic works, to work in gold, in silver, in bronze, in cutting jewels for setting, in carving wood, and to work in all manner of workmanship.'[32]

> *The source of the miracle you are born to do here on earth is that dimension of God on your inside.*

It is the Spirit of God that works through you. No wonder the Bible says, 'God works inside of us both to will and to do of His good pleasure'[33] If you recognise this, you will never compare yourself with or compete with anybody

---

[31] Judges 14:6 NIV
[32] Exodus 31:1-5 NKJV
[33] Philippians 2:13

ever again in your life. You will realise how unique you are and the call of God upon your life such that you will never want anyone else but you.

'So, Pharaoh asked his officials, "Can we find anyone else like this man so obviously filled with the spirit of God?"'[34]

Pharaoh knew that it was the Spirit of God that enabled Joseph to interpret that dream. Who interprets a dream that even the dreamer forgot? It can only come from the Spirit of God. Whenever you recognise the spirit of God on your inside, you realise that no one is like you. You are unique in your own rights if you allow God to express Himself through you. It was that Spirit of God that made Samson kill the lion with his bare hands. That same expression of God was what made David's stone to kill Goliath.

You are reading this right now and you could be wondering if this is also possible for you. My answer is, yes! Everything I have written so far is about you. There's a dimension of God on your inside, there is something that you carry that is not ordinary. It is the dimension of God, and it is the source of all the miracles that God wants to work through you, and I need you to realise that dimension of God on your inside so that you can talk, walk, and think differently and be a blessing to your generation and the ones to come.

Theory of multiple intelligence

I did some findings some years back and found that the closest that anyone has come to explaining the dimension

---

[34] Genesis 41:38 NLT

of God scientifically was the research done by a man called Howard Gardner in the 70s or 80s which he called the Theory of Multiple Intelligence. He came about nine types of intelligence. Many times, we measure people's IQ by their knowledge of logic or mathematics, but this is not a true measure of intelligence, according to Howard Gardener. It is impossible to measure the Spirit of God by any man-made IQ test.

Howard Gardner discovered that men can be smart in broadly nine ways:

1. Naturalist Intelligence

These people are nature-smart. They could distinguish living things – plants, animals, etc., as well as be able to sense other features in our natural world like clouds, rock configuration, flowers, etc. These people could just fall in love with nature and do things with nature.

These are our botanists, farmers, and gardeners. They love nature and do it with so much joy and passion. They may not understand statistics and mathematics, but they know nature so well.

2. Musical Intelligence

These are the Mozarts and the Beethovens of our world. If you are in Christendom, you must have listened to Don Moen, Ron Kenoly, Travis Greene, Nathaniel Bassey, and some of these amazing people. You just listen to them sing or play an instrument and you are awestruck. It's like God is playing an instrument through them. You are experiencing God through them.

When I was at the University, we had a young man in the choir who could pick the key to any song just by listening to the first three words. He was that gifted. It was incredible. I was an amateur keyboardist then, and when people sang, it would take me about 30 seconds to a minute to try to figure out what key they were on, but the young man did not have to do that. He was musically intelligent and gifted.

3. Logical and Mathematical Intelligence

These are people who we think are perhaps the smartest in school because this is majorly the type of intelligence that we often measure people by in school. We usually get it wrong because these people are smart, but they are only smart in an area. It is the dimension of God on their inside that gives them the ability to calculate, quantify and consider hypotheses, laws, logic, and all kinds of statistics and they can do it with so much zest and joy.

These are the Mathematicians, Scientists, and Detectives. They pay so much attention to detail, and they can draw logical conclusions when the facts and numbers are presented.

4. Existential Intelligence

These people are existentially intelligent and have the capacity to tackle deep questions about human existence, life, and the meaning of life or purpose. They can articulate and give explanations as to why we live, why we die and so many others. Some of the ancient Greek Philosophers, the likes of Aristotle, Socrates, and Plato were renowned for this type of intelligence.

These days, some of our pastors, coaches, and philosophers are gifted with this ability. They could think deeply and provide answers to questions about human existence and work miracles in that dimension.

5. Interpersonal Intelligence

These are people who could interact effectively with other people. While you could be struggling to introduce yourself to just one person in the room, they had already made ten friends in the same room they didn't know anyone before. They have effective verbal and nonverbal communication skills; they can denote the distinction between people and know their moods in such a way that they are able to entertain and relate with different people and do it with so much joy.

These are our teachers, actors, politicians, social workers, etc. And they do it with so much joy, especially those who are gifted to do it, not those who are doing it to make a living.

6. Bodily or Kinaesthetic Intelligence

These are people who have an unusual ability to coordinate their minds and their body movements. These are athletes, dancers, etc. When you watch Lionel Messi and Cristiano Ronaldo playing football, it is as if God was on the field of play. They do things those ordinary players cannot do; they score goals that ordinary players cannot score. They just look like they are in their own realm.

These are some of our doctors or surgeons as well. They know how to manipulate the human body to be able to work miracles and solve problems. It's a dimension of God on their inside.

7. Linguistic Intelligence

These people are language smart; they can think clearly and express themselves in words. Some of these kinds of people speak several languages, and they can share human competence through novels, poems, and articles.

If you listen to the former president of the United States, President Barack Obama speak, you will recognise this ability in him. It is often said that he's so gifted that even people who do not like him still enjoy listening to him. He was so good with words and expresses himself with such jaw-dropping dexterity and prowess.

8. Intrapersonal Intelligence

These people have the capacity to understand their own thoughts and feelings and use this understanding to plan and direct their lives. I remember a student colleague some years ago who did a doctoral thesis on herself after having studied herself for three years. She won an award for her outstanding work. What an ability!

Imagine trying to study your life and understand your thoughts just because you have a friend with this level of intelligence. Please, don't even try to compare yourself with such a friend, otherwise, you might start thinking you are hopelessly stupid. Realise and know it is a gift from God, and they are usually self-motivated, self-aware, and could control their own feelings.

9. Spatial Intelligence

These people think in 3-dimension. Talking about architects, sailors, pilots, sculptors, and painters. They are artistic, and they could manipulate graphics as well as take excellent photos. I often joke that when this set of people take photos of you and you don't look good in them, then taking photographs is not your thing.

The point I am trying to make is that there is a dimension of God on your inside, don't take it for granted. God is counting on you to be an expression of His Spirit. Remember, 'There is a spirit in man and the breath of the Almighty gives him understanding'[35]

---

[35] Job 32:8

ACTIVATE THE MIRACLE-WORKING POWER

To activate the miracle-working power, you must first realise that there is power inside of you. Without this realisation, you will never be able to avail the power.

'Now to Him who is able to do exceedingly abundantly above all that we ask or think, according to the power that works in us'[36]

In other words, the miracle God wants to do through you is according to the power that works inside of you. So, there is a power at work inside of you, and you shouldn't take that power for granted because, according to that scripture, it has the capacity to do exceedingly abundantly above what you can think or ask. In other words, with this power at work in you, you can do miracles that are beyond your wildest imagination.

When God was telling Abraham that he was going to have a son, he couldn't comprehend it; it was way beyond his wildest dreams because he was already over 90 years of age. He thought it was naturally impossible. Of course, he was right. Naturally speaking, there was no way Abraham could have a child at that age. But we're speaking of a miracle here – suspension of natural laws and thinking. God looked at him and said, 'I am the God of all flesh, is there anything too hard for me to do?' God was calling

---

[36] Ephesians 3:20 NKJV

forth the power already at work in Abraham that he was unconscious of at the time. You know the rest of the story! The power at work in Abraham eventually made the miracle possible. Isaac was born and all of God's promises became activated through that miracle.

When you possess this realisation that you carry an extraordinary power at work in you, what do you do? The answer is 'start where you are.' Yes, begin to avail that power, and touch lives, one person at a time.

One of my students once asked me, 'I know what God wants me to do but I don't know how to go about it. What do I do?' I told him to start exactly where he was. I emphasised that he began with what he had and where he was, one person at a time. I want to say the same thing to you as well – begin where you are now, with what you have, and start touching lives one person at a time. It's not too late to begin. It is not too early either. You can serve where you are, with what you have. This is the key to activating the miracle-working power at work in you.

I keep reverting to this example because it's so compelling. Again, when Peter and John got to the temple, they didn't have money, so they didn't give the lame man at the Beautiful Gate money but what they gave to him was way more than money. Now, the guy could rise, walk, work, and earn his own money which he was not able to do before. Now he had the freedom to move about but if they had given him money, he would have probably been stuck there, finished the money, and kept begging for more money, in a continuous and endless cycle of survival. With the miracles God is set to do through the power at work in you, you will set people free just like Peter and John. The freedom they will receive will deliver them completely from the shackles of their predicaments. You must activate this power.

You don't need your situation to change before you start, you don't need a lot of money for you to start. I know a lot of people who God has told to start something, and they are waiting to get ready. Do you know that being ready is a myth? You will never be ready for what God has called you to do. Take that statement and write it down where you will see it every single day.

YOU WILL NEVER FEEL FULLY READY FOR WHAT GOD HAS CALLED YOU TO DO

This is the very essence of faith, such that even when you don't feel ready or qualified, you say, 'Lord, send me and I will go for you.' Again, you don't need money to start. You may not need people or any material resources to start but I assure you, what you need is faith. Faith is not when you can see the entire journey, faith is when you only see one step and you decide to go all the way. Have you not read in the scriptures that 'Faith is the substance of things hoped for, the evidence of things not seen?'[37] You haven't seen it all. Logically, it's not working out, but you believe God is with you, and you trust that the One who has called you is faithful. This is what faith is all about. Despite the lack of logic, you have evidence of what you don't see outside on your inside – that power at work in you. Again, it sounds crazy but that is what faith is all about.

So, start with what you have, where you are, and start right now. Unless God is telling you to hold on, start right now. Start with one person. If that thing is something that

---

[37] Hebrews 11:1

involves so much money and you need to raise the money, you can start by praying. Start praying, start trusting God, and start talking to some trusted people around you. Money is not always the first place to start. Whatever it is God has called you to do, money is not the first place to start. Where to start is to begin to pray. Where to start is to begin to talk to the right people. Where to start is to begin to nurture and grow the seed in your mind.

> **So, start with what you have, where you are, and start right now.**

'Though your beginning was small, yet your latter end would increase abundantly'[38]

'And though you started with little, you will end with much.'[39]

Do you have a little now? That is all you need to start. That widow of Zarephath had only a little flour for her and her son to eat and die. Yet, Elijah said they should prepare it for him because he understood this principle that little is all you need to work miracles. If you have a little – the five loaves of bread, the jar of oil, a rod in your hands, etc. – you are good to go. With God, the fact that you have something is enough for you to get started. Start with what you have and start where you are.

'But the path of the righteous is like the light of dawn, which shines brighter and brighter until full day'[40]

---

[38] Job 8:7 NKJV
[39] Job 8:7 NLT
[40] Proverbs 4:18 ESV

The light may not be bright today but as you keep going, it keeps shining brighter and brighter. The moment you trust God to get started on that path paved for you by Him and decide to start shining with what you have and where you are. God will make sure you do not remain small. It would keep getting better and bigger. That is all that is required, and your light would begin to shine brighter and brighter until full day. No wonder the Bible says, 'The glory of the latter shall be more than the former'[41] This is how to activate the miracle-working power on your inside – you must start with what you have and where you are. Start with one person, you don't need to be big or have a multitude gathered to start.

The power is a seed

The power at work in you is a seed. Every time God wants to start something, He deposits a seed. The interesting thing about a seed is the fact that when it goes into the ground, it dies. Death often seems like the end until a few days later when a new life comes out of the dead seed. This is the paradox of a miracle. The power must be committed to the ground by faith – in other words, put to work by faith. Until the seed goes into the ground and dies, the potential of the seed would never be seen. This reminds me of the words of Jesus when He said, 'Very truly I tell you, unless a kernel of wheat falls to the ground and dies, it remains only a single seed. But if it dies, it produces many seeds.[42]' No one would ever witness the miracle-working power within you if you remain in hiding or obscurity. You must commit it to use by faith.

---

[41] Haggai 2:9
[42] John 12:24 NIV

Interestingly, a seed is also very little, so it is easy to despise it, but it is that same seed that ends up becoming a tree that produces more seeds and then becomes a forest. So, do not despise the seed inside of you. That is why Paul advised Timothy, 'Do not let any man despise your youth.'[43] Do not let any man despise your days of little beginning. Do not let anyone despise what you're carrying. Even if it does not seem of much value yet, keep nurturing it and committing it to use by faith.

Here is another illustration Jesus used: 'The Kingdom of Heaven is like a mustard seed planted in a field. It is the smallest of all seeds, but it becomes the largest of garden plants; it grows into a tree, and birds come and make nests in its branches.'[44]

The smallest seed goes into the ground, dies, and grows to become the largest garden plant and birds come to make their nests in its branches. The seed inside of you has a glorious future, the seed inside of you has many destinies connected to it. If you plant it and let it grow through the seasons of obscurity and adversity, if you persevere through these seasons, you will become a massive garden plant that will grow into a tree where birds can make their nests – this means influence. You begin to attract other people who would come to make their nests on your branches.

The Bible says, 'You are the light of the world. A city set on a hill cannot be hidden.'[45] You may be hidden for a while, but you cannot be hidden forever. There is something inside of you that comes out as fine gold – after

---

[43] 1 Timothy 4:12
[44] Matthew 13:31-32 NLT
[45] Matthew 5:14

it goes into the ground, and you come out from the season of obscurity. There is a seed inside of you that works miracles.

Develop and refine the power – practice, service and learning/growth

I also want to let you know that the seed must grow. Some people think the seed will grow automatically, but this is not true. In fact, this is one of the problems I have with most Christians, they just believe that because they are children of God, they will grow automatically. This is a terrible mindset to have. Prayer alone would not help you grow. Prayer is key to growth, but you must also learn principles, you must commit yourself to growth. I love how the Bible puts it, 'A wise man will hear, and will increase learning; and a man of understanding shall attain unto wise counsels.'[46] You must increase your learning. Growth requires intentionality. You must be intentional about your growth – this is how the seed in you would find expression. You must commit daily to growth. Don't ever give an excuse not to grow daily. No excuse is tenable for you not to grow daily. Every single day, you must listen to something positive, read something, and you must hear something from God.

Four Pillars of Growth

1. Your Walk with God

You must spend time with God daily. You must spend time praying and communing with God, praying for the seed inside of you. You must also study the Word of God

---

[46] Proverbs 1:5 KJV

and hear God speak to you through it. This is very germane to your growth.

Consider these scriptures:

'Your own ears will hear him. Right behind you a voice will say, "This is the way you should go," whether to the right or to the left.'[47]

'I keep my eyes always on the Lord. With him at my right hand, I will not be shaken.'[48]

'The steps of a good man are ordered by the Lord, And He delights in his way.'[49]

God wants to lead you but for Him to lead you, you must hear His voice. In all your ways acknowledge Him, you must always want to make sure that you are following God. You must put God at your right hand.

2. The Books You Read

Some people believe that books are not for them, some people even take pride and say, 'It's my nature, I don't really like reading.' It's more like saying, 'I don't really want to be great.' If you want to work miracles, you must commit to learning by books.

Daniel gave us a secret about his life, 'In the first year of his reign **I Daniel understood by books** the number of the years, whereof the word of the LORD came to Jeremiah the prophet, that he would accomplish seventy years in the desolations of Jerusalem'[50]

---

47 Isaiah 30:21 NLT
48 Psalms 16:8 NIV
49 Psalms 37:23 NKJV
50 Daniel 9:2 KJV (Emphasis Added)

He had to read, no wonder he was placed among the princes in a foreign land. Daniel was an avid reader; he was committed to learning. There was a time I was doing a study on Nehemiah, and I realised that he understood history and from his knowledge of history, he knew that it was not normal for the walls of Jerusalem to be down. He got his knowledge of history from reading books.

Never let a day go without you reading a few pages from a book, especially books that help to nurture the seed of the miracle-working power you carry. This is why I keep a library. I intentionally invest in books. I tell my mentees all the time to shop for their greatness by buying books that would help them become great.

3. The Places You Learn

You must be intentional about the places you learn - the conferences you attend, and the podcasts you listen to. Every year, you must make a selection of conferences you attend because the Bible says, 'Faith comes by hearing and hearing by the word of God.'[51] The more of the Word of God that you hear, the more great things that you hear, and the more you nurture the miracle-working seed in you.

4. The People You Learn from

Do you know that 80% of your success in life depends on the people you learn from? Be intentional about the people you surround yourself with. If you surround yourself with failures and negative people or people who don't believe in you, or who are jealous of you, then you probably are not going to get anywhere. You must handpick the people that

---

[51] Romans 10:17

you surround yourself with. People you learn from are the people you must have around you.

> *Remember, it takes growth to work miracles.*

In the first chapter of this book, we said that the greatest miracle in life is the miracle of a changed life. That change begins with your mindset. This is where growth and personal development come in. Be intentional about the people you listen to. There are people I listen to every single day without fail because what you listen to determines where you are going. What you listen to determines whether you are going to have faith or fear. Anything you listen to is either growing your faith or growing your fear. Be intentional about the things that grow your faith.

You must activate the power inside of you, and you can activate that by realising you can start where you are and with what you have. Even though you start small, God can make it bigger than your imagination if you are faithful and diligent. Remember, it takes growth to work miracles.

DESTINIES ARE CONNECTED TO YOUR MIRACLES

Your miracles will attract others to you

I remember a time when a lady came to me and told me that she was suicidal. Anytime I hear the 's-word,' I become very concerned because I was created to help people discover their purpose. I believe that nothing should die unless it fulfils its purpose. Anytime I hear the 's-word,' I am always stirred to swing into action. Such news causes me to feel grief, to weep, and to get angry in my spirit enough to want to do something about it. When this lady told me her story, I was moved. I spent some time with her telling her about the purpose of God for her life. To the glory of God, today, she is alive and no longer suicidal. She is living purposefully today.

Through that situation, I realised that what God has called us to do is very much connected to the lives of others, to the hope that they need and the freedom that they need from the oppression they are under. It is germane for you to enter your miracle-working arena so that you can begin to work miracles that will set people free from every oppression in their lives.

The miracle-working power that God has put in you will attract others to you. When you begin to serve your generation, you begin to enter your miracle-working power arena, you begin to deliver destinies and work miracles, earning you more attraction from people. They will look at you and they will be able to tell that you are different, that you don't move like everybody else, that you don't talk like everybody else, and that there is a power inside of you that is inherent and unique.

'There was a man of the Pharisees, named Nicodemus, a ruler of the Jews: The same came to Jesus by night, and said unto him, Rabbi, we know that thou art a teacher come from God: for no man can do these miracles that thou doest, except God be with him. Jesus answered and said unto him, Verily, verily, I say unto thee, Except a man be born again, he cannot see the kingdom of God.'[52]

The Pharisees in Jesus' time were like His enemy, they never liked Him at all. They would look at Him from afar and when they came near, it was to criticise and nail Him to the cross even before Calvary happened.

The scripture above is the template of what this whole book is about. When you begin to work miracles, when you begin to do what God has called you to do – setting people free and serving your generation – a lot of people will be attracted to you, including the people who supposedly hate you. People will criticise you and not like you, but many of them would come to you by night, they would come to you in secret. They would want to know what makes you tick just as Nicodemus came to Jesus – because he had seen the miracles Jesus was working and His undiluted teaching – to ask how He did what He did. Jesus gave him an answer that I think is worth delving into: *'Except a man be born again, he cannot see the kingdom of God.'* The meaning of Jesus' response is that when men and women get attracted to the miracles you are working, to

---

[52] John 3:1-3 KJV

the things the Spirit of God on your inside is doing outwardly, you point them back to the Kingdom of God. This is what I meant by the expansion of the Kingdom of God. Thousands by thousands as they come, hundreds by hundreds as they come, you point them back to the Kingdom of God. Let them know that unless a man is born again, he can't see the kingdom of God. Many of them would ask how they can do the same things you do, and you let them know unless they accept Jesus into their lives and come into God's kingdom, they won't be able to tap into their miracle-working abilities given by the Spirit of God. Miracles start by identifying with God.

What are the things that Nicodemus saw? He saw the turning of water to wine[53] He also saw the cleansing of the temple, and those were the initial miracles of Jesus. It was not that Jesus had done tonnes of miracles, but he was paying attention and those miracles made a deep impression on him. Even though he was a Pharisee, he knew that those miracles were not ordinary. Only someone who had the Spirit of God could do them. He either couldn't wait till the next morning or to save his face, he just had to come at night. Some people will come to you like that, in secret or in an emergency. There are so many destinies that you need to free through the miracle-working power that God has put on your inside. What Nicodemus was telling Jesus was, 'Excuse me, Sir, you are unique, you stand out, and there is a grace upon your life that is undeniable.' When you begin to do what God has called you to do, you too will experience the same thing. Don't fail the destinies and lives connected to you. The

---

[53] John 2

time has come to discover and begin tapping into the miracle-working power within you.

Your miracles will require you to be different

For your miracles to attract other people, you must separate yourself from the pack. In other words, you must be different. Nicodemus said to Jesus, '*Rabbi, we know that thou art a teacher come from God: for no man can do these miracles that thou doest, except God be with him.*' In other words, what he was trying to say is 'You are different, you are not like everybody else, we have seen some people and your own is different.' If you are going to work miracles, you must embrace your uniqueness, the gifts inside of you, and the purpose of God for your life - this is what makes you unique and stand out from the crowd. And even though you are going to be criticised heavily, please do it. Without separation, you cannot stand for God in this dark world. You cannot talk like the world, walk like everybody else, and still work miracles or expand God's kingdom. You must be different. Do not be afraid to be different. It is okay to be different.

I like how the Bible puts it,

'Come out from among them and be separate, says the Lord. Do not touch what is unclean, and I will receive you. I will be a Father to you, and you shall be My sons and daughters, says the Lord Almighty.'[54]

---

[54] 2 Corinthians 6:17-18 NKJV

> *Your uniqueness is not something to be ashamed of. It is the source of your value.*

I am also reminded of the time Jesus commanded the storm to be still. By the time He was done, the Bible says that everybody fastened their eyes on Him and asked each other 'Who is this? Even the wind and the waves obey him!'[55] The miracle-working power that God has put on your inside has the capacity to separate you from the pack.

Your uniqueness is not something to be ashamed of. It is the source of your value. It is what attracts the destinies you are called to serve to you. Please, don't allow the fear of being persecuted or criticised to make you want to blend with others. You must stand for something. You must stand for the kingdom of God. When you don't stand for something, you fall for everything. God wants you to take a stand as a custodian of His miracle-working power.

Your miracles will lift others

Many people are at their lowest right now, and there are many people who don't know what to do with their lives but when they encounter you, they will encounter the miracle-working power that God has put on your inside, and they become lifted from every miry clay and perils of life. We talked about that earlier, 'And he took him by the right hand and <u>lifted him up</u>, and immediately his feet and ankle bones received strength'[56]

---

[55] Mark 4:41
[56] Acts 3:7 NKJV (Emphasis Added)

Some people are where they are today because they haven't found out about you, and what you're carrying that they desperately need. The day they encounter you, the day they get in touch with you, as Nicodemus got in touch with Jesus, they will be lifted from their horrible pits.

Some people in your family, in your circle of friends, or your community may never come out of poverty until you begin to work the miracles God has destined you to work, or until you begin to walk in the purpose of God for your life and do what God has destined for you to do. Some people are sick right now, sinking into the bottomless pit of depression, addiction, and anxiety, and may never get their healing until you begin to work the miracles that God has asked you to work, or until you start that business that God has asked you to start. You were created and called to lift others and we see that many times when Jesus would heal someone, the Bible would state it clearly that 'Jesus lifted him up.' An example was when Jesus went to the house of Simon's mother-in-law. The Bible says, 'And he came and took her by the hand and <u>lifted her up</u>. Immediately the fever left her, and she ministered unto them'[57] Miracles are meant to lift people.

We see this again when Jesus healed that man that was demon-possessed, the disciples tried and tried but couldn't get it done because they had no faith. The Bible says, *'But Jesus took him by the hand and <u>lifted him up</u>; and he arose.*[58] The miracle-working power that God has put on your inside is meant to lift many people up and you cannot

---

[57] Mark 1:31 KJV (Emphasis Added)
[58] Mark 9:27 KJV (Emphasis Added)

afford to deny those destinies. You must begin to work those miracles so they can be lifted.

Peter undoubtedly learnt this from Jesus, as he can be seen later in scripture lifting people up with the right hand which signifies strength. Peter did the same thing when he raised Dorcas from the dead. 'Then Peter arose and went with them. When he was come, they brought him into the upper chamber: and all the widows stood by him weeping, and shewing the coats and garments which Dorcas made, while she was with them. But Peter put them all forth, and kneeled down, and prayed; and turning him to the body said, Tabitha, arise. And she opened her eyes: and when she saw Peter, she sat up. And he gave her his hand, and <u>lifted her up</u>, and when he had called the saints and widows, presented her alive.[59]

There are many dead circumstances that you will cause to rise if you will begin to work the miracles that God has destined you to work.

When you work the miracles that God has destined you to work, the things you do will be undeniable. Your critics, haters, and people who don't like you will try to gain say and oppose what God is doing through you, but they will fail. Remember that man at the Beautiful Gate, by the time he was healed and lifted, the Bible said he was dancing, leaping, and praising God in joy and the elders of the land saw him and they had to go and call Peter and John to query them, but they couldn't do anything because the miracle-working power was undeniable. The Bible recorded that because of that man, they didn't know what to do with Peter and John. They just had to warn them not

---

[59] Acts 9:39-41 KJV (Emphasis Added)

to do more miracles in the land and let them go because what God does through a man is undeniable. The Spirit and grace of God that is on your inside – that works miracles – is undeniable. This is why you should do the things that God has called you to do.

BARRIERS TO WORKING MIRACLES

While the ability to work miracles is inherent inside of you, you must guard and watch out for things that could affect that ability from manifesting in your life. Many people are not aware of these things I am about to share with you, and as a result, they are living ordinary lives whereas they are supposed to be living a life of dominion.

Follow me as I show you some of these barriers so you can watch their manifestations in your life and what you should do about them, in case they exist in your life already.

Lack of intimacy with god

This is a major barrier to working miracles. If you remember where we started from, I said that it is the Spirit of God on your inside that enables you to work miracles – *'Breath of the Almighty.'*

There is something about that breath. It needs to stay in connection with the source. Anytime a man allows sin to come in between him and God, that man is denying himself of his miracle-working ability. We see that in the Book of Genesis. As soon as the man (male and female) fell into sin, they lost intimacy with God and because of that, struggle entered the world.

Even though man was working before sin came into the picture, he never struggled. He was working without struggle and was able to eat without struggling. Everything man did was like a miracle. But as soon as sin entered the world and created a barrier between man and God, everything became a struggle.

Sin brought a distance between God and man. Whenever there is a lack of intimacy between God and man, man struggles. Have you noticed that every time you don't have a smooth relationship with God, you are in a place of guilt, shame, and condemnation that the devil brings? You start to struggle, and whenever you are in that place, it will be hard for you to function in your purpose and do what God has called you to do.

This is very vital because if you are not careful, you can be intimidated, abused, and oppressed by the devil. It is, therefore, very important to make sure nothing comes between you and God if you must work miracles.

When the army of Israel faced Goliath, they knew God, but they didn't have a relationship with Him. That was why none of them was bold enough to look Goliath in the face and tell him they were part of the army of the Living God. But one 17-year-old boy, called David, came and showed them how it should be done.

He said, 'I am not coming to you in my name, I am coming to you in the name of the Lord, God of Hosts.' He was sure of his intimacy with God that he had to boast about Him and His miracle-working power. Of course, we know how it all ended. He was able to kill Goliath and delivered the entire nation of Israel as a result.

When you have a relationship with God, there is this audacity that comes whenever you face any problem that you are born to solve. You will do it with joy and confidence. No wonder when Peter and John got to that beautiful gate in the case study we have been using all through this book, it was so easy for them to say, 'In the name of Jesus, rise up and walk.' Why? Because they had an intimate relationship with Jesus.

When a man has an intimate relationship with Jesus, he carries the presence of God wherever he goes. So, you can work miracles in your street, place of work, and environment. Anywhere you find yourself, you can work miracles because you are the embodiment of God's presence. Working miracles through His presence is natural when you have intimacy with God. When you carry His presence, your life becomes a natural expression of His miracle-working power.

> *When a man has an intimate relationship with Jesus, he carries the presence of God wherever he goes.*

That was David's secret. In most chapters of the Psalms written by David, you can almost feel the love and intimacy David and God shared from his words.

'The one thing I ask of the LORD--the thing I seek most--is to live in the house of the LORD all the days of my life, delighting in the LORD's perfections and meditating in his Temple.'[60]

---

[60] Psalms 27:4 NLT

You can read his words and almost picture him and God in a tango dance and having a romantic relationship. No wonder God said David was a man after His heart.

Another person that demonstrated intimacy with God was Moses. He told God, 'If you don't go with us personally, don't let us move a step from this place.'[61] Moses enjoyed the presence of God, and he was recorded as a man who saw and spoke to God from mouth to mouth. That is so powerful. Any man that has such a level of intimacy with God will work miracles.

Do not allow any day to pass without consciously measuring your relationship with God and making sure that it is intact. If you are not sure, please return to Him. He says in His Word, 'Come unto me all ye that labour and are heavy laden, I will give you rest...'[62] God gave me a personal revelation of this scripture many years ago, and I always have it at the centre of my heart. He said to me after reading the verse that day, 'No matter what you do, no matter what happens, don't stop coming back to my presence.' Since then, I knew nothing could hold me back from His presence. No matter the guilt, or condemnation I feel, if I can just find my way back into His presence, I'll be restored.

God is constantly seeking men and women who will have a relationship with Him so He can work miracles through them in their various spheres of influence.

---

[61] Exodus 33:15 NLT
[62] Matthew 11:28 KJV

Lack of focus

I believe that one of the strongest weapons of the enemy in this generation is distraction. Distraction has become something that the enemy uses a lot. There are so many people distracted by mundane things, distracted by entertainment, distracted by making money, and living aside the very core of why they were created. If you are distracted, you cannot work miracles.

I often joke about how so many people in our world that God wants to do some great things through their lives, have gone into things that are entirely contrary to their calling or they have become busy chasing things or money up and down. Any time a man loses focus on the things that matter, he loses the matter completely.

I remember the story of Samson; he was doing so well and was working miracles. He tore the lion apart, he was fighting and defeating the enemies. Samson was that man that was so powerful that the enemy could not approach the people of God until he was distracted by Delilah. The moment Delilah stepped into his life, everything took a downward turn.

This is one of the things that the enemy still uses in our time. You will see great men and women, and suddenly distraction just comes in the form of women, men, or money and they are no longer working miracles. They have completely abandoned what they have been called to do. They have pursued the mundane at the expense of the ordained in their lives.

This must not be you because anything you focus on expands. You must be mindful of what you give your focus to. If you give focus to anything, you give power to that thing and the main thing may lose power in your life. Ask yourself, 'What in my life right now is taking most of my attention?'

The key to staying focused in our world is to have your priorities set. So many people don't have their priorities set. What are the five core things that are on the top of your priority list? You must have core priorities. I have my core priorities and I am always intentional about them. There is no way that I will go and give my attention to something else when I need to spend time with God or my family, for instance.

> *If you give focus to anything, you give power to that thing and the main thing may lose power in your life*

I try my best to give my focus to what I am supposed to be focused on because what you focus on does expand. Your feelings go with your focus. You must be intentional about what you focus on. There is a psychological study that talks about how many people think they are multitalented and can do lots of things at a time. But the research has shown us that doing multiple things simultaneously often leads to a lack of efficiency or productivity. The brain cannot do two or three things at the same time. What you are doing when you say you are multitasking is that you are distracting yourself – doing less of something to do more of another thing at that time. So, you are not being productive. Research has also shown that it takes a while for you to focus again on something you have lost focus on.

I love the words of Paul the Apostle,

'Brethren, I count not myself to have apprehended: but this one thing I do, forgetting those things which are behind, and reaching forth unto those things which are before, I press toward the mark for the prize of the high calling of God in Christ Jesus.'[63]

This is one trait every believer must have – focusing on one thing. I am usually very big on this one-thing principle because I have seen it change my life. I remember in 2016 when God revealed to me His purpose for my life, which is to help other people discover their purpose. What I did then was to quit many of the things I was doing that were competing with my life's purpose. At that time, I had a web development company, and I was secretary of a community association in New Zealand. I was all over the place. But the moment I heard that word, I knew I had to be focused and set my priorities right. What I realised was that the moment I quit all of that, my productivity increased and everyone around me started to notice that there was a Purpose Preacher around.

'No, dear brothers and sisters, I am still not all I should be, but I am focusing all my energies on this one thing: Forgetting the past and looking forward to what lies ahead'[64]

Some people are prevented from being focused by their pasts. You cannot keep driving forward while looking in the rear mirror. It is only a matter of time before you will be in an accident. Forget the past, forget everything that makes you bitter. Your focus should be on what is ahead not what is behind. There is nothing God wants to do with

---

[63] Philippians 3:13-14 KJV
[64] Philippians 3:13 NLT

what is behind you, He is after what is ahead of you and that is where your focus should be.

The seduction of the rat race

There was a time I released a post on the internet on the graveyards of purpose. One of the graveyards of purpose is career. A young man saw that post and sent me a direct message saying he knew his purpose; he knew what miracles he ought to be working with his life, but his purpose didn't pay the bills. He worked in an oil company, and he didn't have time for anything else. He asked me what to do. I felt like telling him to quit his job and go and do what God had called him to do, but I told him he knows what to do and he should do it. The Bible says to a person who knows what to do and doesn't do it, it is a sin.[65]

It is amazing how a lot of people in our world, including you reading this, know what to do, they know their purpose, and they know what God wants them to do with their lives, yet they allow the things that will bury their purpose to take pre-eminence over them.

Do not allow the rat race to seduce you. Nothing is fulfilling or of eternal gain in the rat race. Even if your calling is in the marketplace, do not be driven by power, positions, or titles, instead be driven by impact and influence. If you let the rat race seduce you, it is only a matter of time before you will lose yourself, if there is an uncertainty or crisis. I always tell people this, 'Do not allow your career to come before your purpose.' No one can sack you from your purpose, but you can be sacked from your job or career. Your entire company can go bankrupt, they

---

[65] James 4:17

could be downsizing, and you may be one of the first persons to be let go. You must understand that your purpose is the only security that God has given you in this world. There is no other security anywhere else other than the purpose of God for your life.

> *Do not allow the rat race to seduce you.*
> *Nothing is fulfilling or of eternal gain*
> *in the rat race.*

One of the illustrations I like to give to support this is that of the eagle. Just imagine an eagle flapping its wings and flying in the expanse of the sky in all its eminence and glory. Now, imagine if the same eagle was locked up in a cage and could no longer fly beyond the perimeter of the cage. Let's assume that the cage is golden and glitters very brightly and beautifully. Does it change the fact that the eagle can no longer flap its wings and express its full glory? This is what employment does to many people. Employment is sometimes the enticing, seductive golden cage that restricts people from flying high, fulfilling their purpose, or maximising their potential. Let me offer you more perspectives; in the cage, the eagle is only able to eat what it is given to eat, whereas when flying in all the expanse of the sky with freedom, the eagle can fly to any mountain of its choice, and if it likes, it comes down to the valley or picks up prey in the waters. You get to see a limited eagle in a cage and an unlimited one when it is free!

If you allow yourself to be seduced and caged in the rat race, you would be clipping your wings. So many people have allowed their careers to bury their purpose, this must not be you. It does not matter if you win in a rat race, you are still a rat. The best you can be is a big rat.

I was reading *40 Days to the Work You Love*, a book by Dan Miller and he said it is an insult to rats to say men are in a rat race because rats don't stay in a race where there is no cheese. The moment you take away the cheese, the rat goes away but you will find many human beings in a race where there are no benefits just because they don't want to lose their security. There is no security outside your life's purpose. Nothing in life can promise you more security than the purpose of God for your life.

I often say, do not let anything that can be taken from you determine your self-worth. If you make your job a determinant of your self-worth, it is only a matter of time, you will be frustrated. I think it is suicidal to make anything that can be taken from you the source of your self-worth because the moment it is taken away, you will feel very devalued and worthless.

Lack of commitment to processes

There are so many people willing to work miracles, but they are not willing to pay the price of commitment to the process. There is always a process involved at every stage of our walk with God that requires our commitment. I said in one of the chapters before that God is always looking for who will put their hands up when He asks, 'Who shall I send?' When you put your hand up, remember there is a price to pay.

You must commit to the process; you can't belong to the group of people who love change but are unwilling to commit to change. I was trying to lose weight recently and I realised that there is so much price to pay to lose weight

– I have got to exercise daily, watch what I eat, and be intentional about when I eat and how I eat. There is always a price to pay for greatness and if we are going to work miracles, we must commit to pay that price.

Many people do not understand that before gold can become valuable in a shop, it must be tried by fire. It must be committed to the fiery furnace – thousands of degrees Celsius of heat – for it to be refined and purified. So many people want to be great and valuable, but they don't want to be refined and purified, they don't want to go through the process.

'And Jesus grew in wisdom and stature, and in favour with God and men.'[66]

Every time I read that scripture, I often wonder why Jesus (who is God) does have to grow. I was asking God that question in my meditation one day and God said, 'Whatever I have called you to do, you have to grow into it.' No wonder the Bible says, 'He makes everything beautiful in his time.'[67] Before that time, growth and maturity must take place. If we are not patient and committed to His timing, we will lose the beauty of His plans and purpose for us. In our timing, God may seem slow but that is not true. His ways are not our ways. Just as the Bible succinctly puts it, 'For my thoughts are not your thoughts, neither are your ways my ways, saith the LORD. For as the heavens are higher than the earth, so are my ways higher than your ways, and my thoughts than your thoughts.' His ways, His processes, are way different from

---

[66] Luke 2:52 NIV
[67] Ecclesiastes 3:11

ours. We must trust Him and commit to His process so that, in the end, all things are made beautiful for us.

God's process comes with learning, discipline, perseverance, and practice. You must commit to all the things that will make you into who God has created and called you to be. Because you will have to grow into everything God has created you to be. God makes everything beautiful in His own time. You must allow time. One of the functions of time is process, practice, and commitment. God is not a magician, and that is why Jesus himself had to grow. For thirty years, we didn't hear anything about Jesus doing any miracle even though He was the Messiah because He was committed to growing in stature, wisdom, and favour with God and men. If Jesus grew, then you too must grow.

> *God's process comes with learning, discipline, perseverance, and practice.*

BARRIERS TO WORKING MIRACLES – II

Ignorance of principles

I got to realise some years ago that principles mean 'the first law' i.e. *'Pri' means first and 'Ciples' means laws.*

Who made the first law? God in heaven. This is why we call them principles; they exist before every other law. Every other law is subject to God's first laws. Any law that is not rooted in God's laws will automatically fail. This is why principles are so important. If we are going to work miracles, we must understand that principles are God's laws concerning the sphere of life we have been called into.

Some Christians are very lazy. Though they are children of God who are filled with the Spirit of God, they are ignorant or ignore principles. It is impossible to ignore principles and work miracles because principles sustain miracles. Whenever a man ignores principles, he will never be able to do the extraordinary. That man will find it very hard to have God intervene in his affairs because God honours His principles.

God's instructions to Joshua when he was appointed the leader of God's people was, 'Keep this Book of the Law always on your lips; meditate on it day and night, so that you may be careful to do everything written in it. Then you will be prosperous and successful.[68] Miracles can be a one-off event, but consistent success demands obedience to laws/principles. God had to remind Joshua that the task ahead of him would require consistent success and the only way he was going to get that would be to digest God's laws, keep them in his heart day and night, and most importantly practise them.

I will bow down toward your holy temple and will praise your name for your love and your faithfulness, for you have exalted above all things your name and your word.[69]

God is so holy that He ensures that everything works in accordance with His laws. When a man knows God's laws, he leads in every area of life because God honours His laws. Ignoring God's laws is to your detriment, but embracing them will bring you tremendous success in all your endeavours.

Jesus understood this key when He said,

'Do not think that I have come to abolish the Law or the Prophets; I have not come to abolish them but to fulfil them. I tell you the truth, until heaven and earth disappear, not the smallest letter, not the least stroke of a pen, will by any means disappear from the Law until everything is accomplished'[70]

If you are going to work miracles, you must be aware of the laws that are operating in the realm that God has called you to work miracles in. If you are working in the entertainment industry, you must be conversant with the

---

[68] Joshua 1:8 NIV
[69] Psalms 138:2 NIV
[70] Matthew 5:17-18 NIV

laws of God concerning the industry. This is how you uniquely do yours.

No one fulfils God's laws and lives an ordinary life because that is literally how to work miracles. We only work miracles when we are obeying God's laws. Laws are the rules that govern how things are meant to function. When a man understands the rules that God has put in place for things to function, everything will answer to him.

We have two kinds of laws – spiritual and natural laws. Spiritual laws include the laws of sowing and reaping, the law of giving, the law of process, the law of faith, and so on. Peter walked on water and made history because he obeyed the law of faith. So many people believe Peter walked on water, no! Peter simply walked on the word 'come' that Jesus spoke. When you walk on the Word, you are obeying the law of faith. Faith means ignoring what you see and acting on what God said. That was what Peter did. And if he did that, he defied the natural law of sinking. But as soon as he became afraid because of the storm around him, he subjected himself to natural laws, and he began to sink. Please note that fear is the opposite of faith.

Whenever a man honours the laws of God, he works miracles. If you want to work miracles in whatever sphere of life that God has called you into right now, find out the laws that God has established in that area. As soon as you find them out and begin to obey them, you will begin to do extraordinary things.

> *Whenever a man honours the laws of God, he works miracles.*

There are also natural laws which include the law of gravity, the laws of motion and electricity, etc. I believe there are natural laws in different spheres of life like marketing, etc. that many believers are too lazy to study. If you are too lazy to study these laws, it will be difficult to do exploits in your field. For instance, when you understand how marketing works, it will just work for you. Many churches could be growing right now but the people are just praying without understanding the principles that will birth church growth. These are some things that you cannot ignore and expect to work miracles.

My good friend, Debola Deji Kurunmi, once said, 'God is not religious.' God is looking for any man who obeys His principles. When a man honours God's principles, God intervenes. If you want God to do miracles in your life, what you should be doing is working the principles that are around the miracles you desire. Remember that principles sustain miracles.

Many people today want miracles without working principles. You must understand that God doesn't bend His principles. If you want financial miracles, learn the principles within the financial realm. Similarly, if you want miracles in your career, you must learn the principles within the realm of your career. Nothing just happens!

'Then I said, "But what can we expect from the poor? They are ignorant. They don't know the ways of the LORD. They don't understand God's laws"'[71]

If a man does not know the principles of God, he will be poor. I don't care who you are, what I know is that some principles are universal, and they are there for everyone.

---

[71] Jeremiah 5:4 NLT (Emphasis Added)

Whether you are born again or not, if you understand the laws of giving and the law of sowing and reaping, they will work for you.

'So, I will go and speak to their leaders. Surely, they know the ways of the Lord and understand God's laws…'[72]

This means that anyone knowledgeable about the principles of God will become a leader in their field. If you want to work miracles, if you want to lead in that area of life you have been called into, then you must be aware of the laws and principles of God. Ignoring principles is a major barrier to working miracles.

Self-devaluation

Self-devaluation is when 'a person characterises themselves, an object, or another person as completely flawed, worthless, or as having exaggerated negative qualities'[73]. One of the reasons why many people devalue themselves or characterise themselves as completely flawed is because they are ignorant of who they are.

I've always believed that Satan's greatest fear is that you would find your identity in God and believe it. He knows that the day you find out who you truly are, who God has destined you to be, and believe it, he no longer has power over you. The day you know who God has created and called you to be and you believe it, the devil is in trouble. The reason why many children of God devalue and underestimate themselves is that they have no idea of who God created and called them to be. When a man knows

---

[72] Jeremiah 5:5 NLT (Emphasis Added)

[73] Source: https://www.verywellmind.com/devaluation-and-idealization-in-bpd-425291

who he is in God, that man is full of faith, zest, power, and energy.

Jesus asked His disciples who they thought He was, and there were all kinds of opinions, some said Jeremiah, some said John the Baptist, some said Elijah, but Simon Peter said, 'You are Christ, the son of the living God.' Jesus replied that it was God who revealed it to him and not flesh and blood. We can learn so many lessons from that story, including that no one's identity can be guessed or speculated. All the suggestions the disciples had about the identity of Jesus were false except for the one revealed by God. In other words, your identity can only be revealed by God. You should never rely on men to tell you who you are! They will always get it wrong. After Peter revealed that Jesus is the Son of God, what Jesus said next is worth meditating on:

'And I say also unto thee, that thou art Peter, and upon this rock I will build my church; and the gates of hell shall not prevail against it.'[74]

That revelation that Peter had of Jesus birthed the revelation or declaration of his own identity. Jesus revealed Peter's real identity as 'Cephas' - the rock upon which the church will be built. No wonder Peter was used by God mightily in the early church. To really know who you are in God, you must get a revelation of who God is. You must have a direct encounter with God. And when you find your identity in Christ, you will never doubt or underestimate yourself anymore. When a man knows who he is, he will do the extraordinary, and the miracles he had been destined to do. This reminds me of the story of Jacob who

---

[74] Matthew 16:18 KJV

wrestled with God and after that encounter, his name was changed and God said,

'Thy name shall be called no more Jacob, but Israel: for as a prince hast thou power with God and with men, and hast prevailed.'[75]

To know who you are is to get into God's Word about you.

Before that encounter, Jacob was a cheat! The value of his life was reduced to being a defrauder. He had duped his brother Esau and was running away from him. However, from that day God revealed his identity to him, his life changed for good. He was no longer devaluing himself; he came to the realisation that he was indeed the seed that was prophesied to birth a nation.

To know who you are is to get into God's Word about you. When you know the truth of God's Word about you and your identity, you will no longer devalue yourself. You will never be able to think of yourself any less than who God says you are. The issue with many believers is they have consumed the news too much or listened excessively to men's labels about them, and have believed them; as a result, they are not able to discern their identity in God. Stop listening to who the devil says you are, instead start listening and reading about who God says you are. Your value is in who God says you are. It is not in who men say you are, or in the labels they give you, it is inherent in your God-given identity.

---

[75] Genesis 32:28 KJV

Lack of accountability

Working miracles require you to be under authority. The order in which God lifts often requires submission and accountability. Mantles are not stumbled upon; they are deliberately passed from hand to hand. God is a God of order. Many people don't want to submit themselves to any form of authority. If a man thinks he is bigger than authority, that man will not amount to anything or work miracles. I believe very strongly that our generation is in dire need of men and women who are accountable - accountable to God and accountable to people. Men and women who are not like Saul who did not want to be accountable to the prophet of God. Men and women who are not like the sons of Eli – Hophni and Phinehas – who did not want to be accountable to anybody, but just wanted to do things on their own terms and outside of God's laws and principles. If they are not careful, those who lack accountability will soon be smitten by God Himself.

If you want to work miracles, you must submit yourself to the authority that God has put you under. At a point, even Jesus had to submit Himself to authority when He came to earth. There was a time he had to be baptised by John the Baptist. John the Baptist wanted Jesus to baptise him instead, but Jesus obeyed this principle even though he was the Son of God. If Jesus could submit to authority and be accountable, then we too must learn to submit and be accountable.

I came to realise that the baptism by John the Baptist was a declaration of the assignment of Jesus or rather a confirmation of the purpose of Christ because the Bible says,

'But the Pharisees and the experts in the law rejected God's purpose for themselves, because they had not been baptised by John'[76]

That means that if Jesus had not allowed John the Baptist to baptise Him, He would have rejected the purpose of God for His life. He would not have been able to start or continue His ministry. God wouldn't have been pleased with Him and He would not have been able to work the miracles that he had been destined for. If you want to fulfil the purpose of God for your life, in which the miracles God has destined for you to wrought lies, you will need to submit yourself to the authorities of those God has put you under.

Fear

Fear is one of the barriers to working miracles. Any man that is captured by fear is in bondage.

The Bible says, 'For ye have not received the spirit of bondage again to fear; but ye have received the Spirit of adoption, whereby we cry, Abba, Father.'[77]

Did you notice that in that scripture fear is a spirit; not just that, it is the spirit of bondage. Any man that is ruled by fear is in bondage and is enslaved. God has delivered us from slavery so we can be true sons. The Bible warns us, 'So Christ has truly set us free. Now make sure that you stay free, and don't get tied up again in slavery to the law.'[78] God has delivered you from slavery, don't keep putting yourself in bondage by living in perpetual fear.

---

[76] Luke 7:30 NIV
[77] Romans 8:5 KJV
[78] Galatians 5:1

'For God hath not given us the spirit of fear; but of power, and of love, and of a sound mind.'[79]

Fear is not a spirit from God! If it is not from God, it is from the devil. This is why you must not entertain it in your life. One of the major weapons of the enemy is to inject the spirit of fear into people. And if you are afraid or have the spirit of fear ruling you, you will never be able to work miracles, nor will you be able to do what God has called you to do. Just imagine that Peter and John were afraid to pray for that man at the Beautiful Gate, nothing would have happened and there would have been no record of that miracle. Imagine if the woman with the alabaster box was afraid and did not pour her oil on Jesus. We also saw that as soon as Peter was afraid, he started to sink.

> *God is counting on you and there are so many destinies connected to you.*

Any man that does not know who he is will live in the bondage of who he is not. Any man that does not know what he possesses in God will live in the bondage of what he does not have. You must not let fear hold you back, don't let fear tell you what you cannot do. Don't let fear relegate your miracle-working power to the background. God is counting on you and there are so many destinies connected to you.

Relationships

The right relationship is a major ingredient to working miracles. There are people we move with who stir up in us

---

[79] 2 Timothy 1:7 KJV

our miracle-working abilities and there are those we walk with who will kill it.

The Bible says, 'As iron sharpens iron, so one person sharpens another.'[80] The people in your life are either sharpening you or dulling you. If you are going to work miracles, then you must learn to relate and move with miracle workers. You must learn to relate with people who know who they are in God and have discovered their miracle-working potential.

In that scripture we have used all over this book, the Bible tells us that Peter and John were going to the temple together. We could see an association that brought about the miracle of the Beautiful Gate we are still talking about thousands of years after. Imagine with me that Peter was convinced he could do the miracle, but John began to discourage him. Perhaps when Peter said to the lame man, 'Silver and gold I do not have, but what I do have I give you,' John interrupted and said, 'What else do you have to give? You better let's leave here before you embarrass yourself.' Peter could have left the place discouraged. There are so many things God wants to do through you, but could your association be limiting His move in your life?

I'm also reminded of the story of Paul and Silas who were both captured following their great work in a city on their way to Macedonia. They were put in prison, bound - hands and feet in chains. But the Bible says, 'About midnight Paul and Silas were praying and singing hymns to God, and the other prisoners were listening to them. Suddenly there was such a violent earthquake that the foundations of the prison were shaken. At once all the

---

[80] Proverbs 27:17

prison doors flew open, and everyone's chains came loose.'[81] Did you notice both men started singing and praying together? It was not a case of one person praying and the other grumbling or complaining. They were in it together, and eventually, God sent an earthquake to deliver them.

I could tell you lots of stories to relay this point from the Bible, but I want to share a personal one with you. Some years ago, my friend – Dr Niyi Borire – and I were speaking over the phone about our desire to do virtual meetings that will gather thousands of people. We believe God was inspiring us to do these meetings, however, at the time we could not afford the visions in our hearts. We were inspiring and sharpening each other to believe it was possible, and we didn't hold back. Just two years later, we started seeing some of those things come to pass. We started holding those events. For one, we brought the renowned Nick Vujicic. For another, we had John Maxwell. Talk about the power of relationships to work miracles.

Who are your friends? Are they stirring up your miracle-working potential or are they putting you down?

---

[81] Acts 16:25-26 NIV

DON'T FRUSTRATE GOD'S GRACE

Do not waste the grace of god

God gave us grace so that we can bring Him glory. I remember Apostle Paul declaring boldly to the Corinthian church that the grace of God in his life was not in vain.[82] What a declaration! We too must have the desire to make such a declaration in our generation. In fact, we must always pray, 'May I not frustrate the grace of God upon my life.' The truth is any life that is not bringing God glory is frustrating the grace of God.

This is why any time a man keeps the right posture of using the grace of God upon his life, he is sending glory to heaven. As said earlier, glory means the full weight or full expression of God in a man. So, whatever you are sent here to do or whenever you are working miracles doing what God wants you to do, what you are doing is giving God expression and full display in your life.

One of the ultimate reasons for working miracles is to bring God glory. The word 'glory' which is transliterated as '*kabod*' in the Old Testament, and 'doxa' in the New Testament, also means the full expression of the quality and characteristics of God's nature on our inside. Jesus was the best expression of God's glory on earth because He came to fulfil God's glory on earth.

---

[82] 1 Corinthians 15:10

In the very same way, if you and I are doing what God has called us to do, we will become wonderful expressions of the very nature and characteristics of God. Working miracles and doing good works – that God has before ordained for us to do[83] – become what gives God glory. God is counting on you.

God wants us to have influence beyond our lifetimes

It is myopic to live oblivious of your legacy. It's myopic to limit your life to the confines of your lifetime. There is so much more God wants for you beyond your lifetime. God wants you to operate at the realm or frequency of eternity. Whenever a man is working miracles, he is living beyond his lifetime. For him, it is not about the rat race or making money but about influence beyond his lifetime. People like this do not always find it easy but they are able to withstand the pressures of life. They can withstand tough times.

Just like the words of Viktor E. Frankl, 'Any man that has a why, can bear anyhow,' when you see a man that understands the nature of his calling and is doing what God has called him to do, living beyond the span of his lifetime, you will see him always work miracles.

God wants us to have influence because when we have it, we are able to attract people into the kingdom. What is influence? Influence is the capacity to cause people to make a change without coercion or forcing them. When a man has influence, he will populate heaven and depopulate hell. That is what God wants you to do. God wants you to bring people to the kingdom and the Bible tells us that there is a

---

[83] Ephesians 2:10

reward for that in heaven. The Bible also tells us about the crown of rejoicing which is the reward for anybody who wins souls.

'For what is our hope, or joy, or crown of rejoicing? Are not even ye in the presence of our Lord Jesus Christ at his coming?'[84]

> *Those who populate the kingdom of God will never have their names fade away from history, either in heaven or here on earth.*

Paul was telling his spiritual sons and daughters in Thessalonica the rewards of working miracles and using them to bring souls into the kingdom of God. You are setting yourself up for the crown of rejoicing.

'And they that be wise shall shine as the brightness of the firmament; and they that turn many to righteousness as the stars for ever and ever.'[85]

Those who populate the kingdom of God will never have their names fade away from history, either in heaven or here on earth. It pays to work the miracles that God has called you here to work.

God is not unrighteous

'For God is not unrighteous to forget your work and labour of love, which ye have shewed toward his name, in that ye have ministered to the saints, and do minister.'[86]

---

[84] 1 Thessalonians 2:19 KJV
[85] Daniel 12:3 KJV
[86] Hebrews 6:10 KJV

Whenever you do what God has called you to do, He rewards you. He is not unrighteous. He is a faithful God and a rewarder of those that diligently seek Him.

'Holding forth the word of life; that I may rejoice in the day of Christ, that I have not run in vain, neither laboured in vain.'[87]

It is very important to hold on to what you have been called to do because when you do, you will not run in vain. It is a dangerous thing to run the race that is set before us in vain.

God pays good wages

'The harvesters are paid good wages, and the fruit they harvest is people brought to eternal life. What joy awaits both the planter and the harvester alike!'[88]

> *God pays with grace and glory; man*
> *pays with money*

God doesn't forget your labour; He pays good wages. I need you to know this because there are times when you want to work miracles and people will tell you, 'What are you going to gain from all of this? Is it not better if you just get a job?' Don't let them discourage you. Let them know that God pays good wages. The interesting thing is that God doesn't pay the way man pays. God pays with grace and glory; man pays with money. Whenever God pays in glory, you cannot use man's standard to quantify it.

---

[87] Philippians 2:16 KJV
[88] John 4:36 NLT

Miracles should be an outflow of your intimacy with god

It is good to work miracles but let them be an outflow of your relationship or intimacy with God. Jesus Christ shows us a perfect model. When we work miracles that are not an outflow of our relationship with God, we are wasting our time. When you work miracles as an outflow of your relationship with God and His presence, it means He knows you and you know Him.

Jesus spoke about people who work miracles in His name, yet He doesn't know or recognise them as His own,

'On that last Day many will call me Lord. They will say, 'Lord, Lord, by the power of your name we spoke for God. And by your name we forced out demons and did many miracles.' Then I will tell those people clearly, 'Get away from me, you people who do wrong. I never knew you.'[89]

Don't be so carried away by the desire to work miracles that you lose your desire to know God and to be known by Him. Just recently, I shared on my Instagram handle something the man of God Jentezen Franklin said. According to him, 'Our ultimate glory is to know God and be known by God.' May we never be told that we are not known by God.

'Watch out, so that you do not lose the prize for which we have been working so hard. Be diligent so that you will receive your full reward.'[90]

---

[89] Matthew 7:22-23 (Paraphrased)
[90] 2 John 1:8 NLT

Sin is the only thing that can cut you off from the full reward. Let us look ahead for the full reward of our calling in Christ Jesus. Let us keep pressing for the mark of the high calling and not allow sin to hold us back.

You must work miracles and you must get the full wage of working miracles from God. You must be the full expression of God here on earth and make it to heaven gloriously.

CONCLUSION

There is an expectation of God on your life to work miracles through the gifts He has given to you. Always remember, those gifts are an extension of the grace of God on your life, which means, every time you choose to do what God has called you to do, you are allowing God to express Himself through you.

The expressions of God through you blesses lives, inspires destinies, and offer hope to many. This is why you cannot afford to watch what God has placed in you to die without expression. One of my favourite quotes by Dr Myles Munroe is, "Live Fully, Die Empty". I am convinced that as believers, this should be our mandate. We must be intentional about leaving everything God has deposited inside of us here on earth. We are not going to use our gifts in heaven, we were given to bless lives and cover the earth with God's glory through using them.

Please shun all your excuses. Never for once entertain the excuse that you are not good enough or not qualified. Remember, God does not call the qualified, he qualifies the called. By man's standard, no one is qualified for God's calling, but God's ways are not our ways. He does not see as man sees. I am reminded of when the Prophet Samuel was asked to go anoint the next king of Israel in the house of Jesse. When Samuel saw the first sons of Jesse, He was almost beyond convinced that they were the ones. One after the other, God rejected them all till he got to David. In fact, what God said is worth studying – "Do not consider his appearance or his height, for I have rejected him. The Lord does not look at the things people look at.

People look at the outward appearance, but the Lord looks at the heart[91]". In other words, God's way of qualifying people is not the way we humans qualify people. God is more interested in the heart. If you have been called and gifted by God, it means, He sees your heart, and has qualified you to do what He has called you to do. Do not let anything hold you back.

Also, do not allow fear to get the best of you. The man with the one talent[92] said, "I was afraid and went and hid your gold in the ground". When you allow fear to rule you, it will dominate you and make you an unprofitable servant. Anytime you feel fear, remember the word of God that says, "For God has not given us a spirit of fear and timidity, but of power, love and self-discipline"[93], and confess it daily till you feel the fear no more. God wants us to be courageous and it is only when we're courageous that we can do miracle. It takes courage to do miracles in a world where very few people believe in you, and you sometimes doubt yourself. Courage is not the absence of fear but move on despite the fear. In other words, it is normal to feel fear, what is not normal is to allow it to stop you in your tracks and make you timid where the fulfilment of your calling is concerned.

I love the words of God to Joshua after the death of Moses and it is a scripture you should hold to heart as well. He said, "This is my command—be strong and courageous! Do not be afraid or discouraged. For the LORD your God is with you wherever you go."[94] Take it

---

[91] 1 Samuel 16:7 NIV
[92] Matthew 25:24-25 NIV
[93] 2 Timothy 1:7
[94] Joshua 1:9 NLT

as God's command to you on a daily basis, to be strong and courageous, and to never be afraid or discouraged but to push on doing what God has gifted and called you to do knowing He is with you every step of the way!

So, go ahead and be an expression of God in our generation. Go ahead and rob the grave of your gifts and potential. God ahead and populate heaven and depopulate hell. God is counting on you and generations are waiting to be blessed through you.

I believe in you.